Macmillan Primary Integrated

My Community

STUDENT'S BOOK

TERM 3 GRADE 2

Margaret Bailey • June Blythe-Livingston
Maureen Byfield • Beverley Dinnall • Winnifred Whittaker

MACMILLAN CARIBBEAN

Macmillan Education
Between Towns Road, Oxford OX4 3PP
A division of Macmillan Publishers Limited
Companies and representatives throughout the world

www.macmillan-caribbean.com

ISBN 978-1-4050-5975-6

Text © Pauline Anning, Margaret Bailey, June Blythe-Livingston, Maureen Byfield, Beverley Dinnall, Derek McMonagle and Winnifred Whittaker 2007
Design and illustration © Macmillan Publishers Limited 2007

Editorial consultants: Derek McMonagle and Pauline Anning
First published 2007

All rights reserved; no part of this publication may be reproduced, stored in a retrieval system, transmitted in any form or by any means, electronic, mechanical, photocopying, recording, or otherwise, without the prior written permission of the publishers.

Typeset by Kamae Design
Illustrated by Val Biro, Gillian Chapman/Linden Artists, Jim Eldridge/Beehive Illustration, Robin Lawrie/Beehive Illustration, Chris Rothero/Beehive Illustration, Tek-Art
Cover design by Jason Billin
Cover photograph by Franz Marzouca

The authors and publishers would like to thank the following for permission to reproduce their photographic material:

Alamy/ Robert Harding Picture Library p35, Alamy/ Michael Dwyer p88, Alamy/ Doug Pearson pp93(mr and bl), Alamy/ Oliver Benn p93(br), Alamy/ David R. Frazier Photolibrary p157(t); Art Directors and trip/ Dave Saunders p36(b); Caribbean Stock Photography pp90, 156(t and b); Corbis/ Jan Butchosky-Houser p36(t), Corbis/ Howard Davies p60; Ecoscene/ Andrew Brown p157(b); Getty Images/ Anne Rippy p154; Jamaica Gleaner p79; Lonely Planet/ Christopher P. Baker p59, Lonely Planet/ Holger Leue p96; Bob Swan pp93(ml), 104; Kingston University of Technology p103.

Printed and bound in Malaysia

2011
10 9 8 7 6 5

Contents

Term 3

13	What is a community?	6
14	What does my community look like?	34
15	Who are the people in my community?	44
16	What are the places in our community that we find interesting?	92
17	Why do we find these places interesting?	112
18	What are the plants and animals in my community?	128
19	How are plants and animals useful?	141
20	How do I care for/protect the plants and animals in my community?	154

For the teacher

Macmillan Primary Integrated Curriculum is the first in a comprehensive series of books covering the requirements of the entire Jamaica primary curriculum. The books have been written by an experienced team of writers who have both an in-depth knowledge of primary education in Jamaica and the ability to present the content in a way which will appeal to young students.

The topics of this book follow the same sequence as in the curriculum document. However, in recognising that, there is a good deal of material to be covered in the time available, and some procedures and activities have been grouped together where the authors thought appropriate, but without losing the essential detail of the curriculum.

The focus questions from the curriculum have been adopted as chapter headings so that the teacher can very easily relate the course content to that of the curriculum. Each topic within a chapter has a component in the Student's Book, the Workbook and the Teacher's Guide.

All written exercises are in the Workbook so the Student's Book is not written on at all and only the Workbook needs to be replaced year on year.

In the Teacher's Guide, comprehensive notes amounting to a suggested lesson plan are given, together with stated aims and objectives, key words, any materials needed for the lesson and details of assessment and evaluation.

In order to provide a truly integrated course, suitable exercises for use in Mathematics and Language Arts Windows have been included in each topic.

The content provides a variety of different sorts of activities which will allow all students to enjoy positive achievement by demonstrating those skills in which they are competent, be they writing, working with materials or performing in some way.

Structure of the series

In the first three years the content is totally integrated with a separate Student's Book and Workbook for each term and a Teacher's Book for each year containing extensive teaching notes for each chapter.

	Student's Books	Workbooks	Teacher's Books
Year 1	Term 1 All About Me Term 2 My Family Term 3 My School	Term 1 All About Me Term 2 My Family Term 3 My School	Teacher's Book 1
Year 2	Term 1 My Body Term 2 Living Together Term 3 My Community	Term 1 My Body Term 2 Living Together Term 3 My Community	Teacher's Book 2
Year 3	Term 1 How Does My Body Work? Term 2 Culture Term 3 My Environment	Term 1 How Does My Body Work? Term 2 Culture Term 3 My Environment	Teacher's Book 3

For Grades 4-6 there are separate books for the different disciplines. The following Macmillan courses have been developed for primary students and teachers in the Caribbean:

- Primary English - *Language Tree* Grades 4-6
- Primary Mathematics - *Bright Sparks* Grades 4-6
- Primary Science - *Bright Ideas* Grades 4-6
- *Primary Social Studies for Jamaica* Grades 4-6 (forthcoming).

For all these courses, each Student's Book has an accompanying Workbook and Teacher's Book.

There is also a wide range of teacher's resources (lesson plans and worksheets) for *Language Tree, Bright Sparks, Bright Ideas* and *Social Studies* that are freely downloadable from the Teacher Resources section of the Macmillan Caribbean website: www.macmillan-caribbean.com .

13 What is a community?

13.1 My community

What is a community?

Hello, I am Tammie. I am eight years old.
I live in Meadowbrook.
Meadowbrook is the name of a place in Kingston.
A lot of adults and children live here.
I think Meadowbrook is a very lovely place to live.

I am Gordon. I am also eight years old.
I live in Happy Grove.
Happy Grove is in the parish of Portland.
It is near the sea so I go to the beach very often.
Tammie is my pen-friend. I saw her name in my school's newspaper. We write to each other very often. We tell each other many things about where we live and the fun things we do.

I am Joudy-Ann. I am also eight years old.
I live in Happy Grove in the parish of St Elizabeth.
I am pen-friends with Tammie and Gordon. I was very excited and surprised when I found out that some places in Jamaica have the same name. I told all my friends at school.

Tammie, Gordon and Joudy-Ann all told you the names of the places where they live. Instead of saying 'places' in which they live we could say 'communities' in which they live.
We all live in a community.

More about communities

The home is the first community.

This is where we first meet other people. These people are our family members.
In the family home, family members live together, work together and have fun together.
A community is a group of people who live and work together.
Family members work in the home and outside the home so that they can provide the things they need to be comfortable.

The next community for many people is the church and then the school.

Communities in Jamaica

Families make up communities.
There are many communities in Jamaica.
Some of these communities are alike while some are different.

Everyone belongs to a community.
Our island is made up of parishes.
These parishes have many small communities.

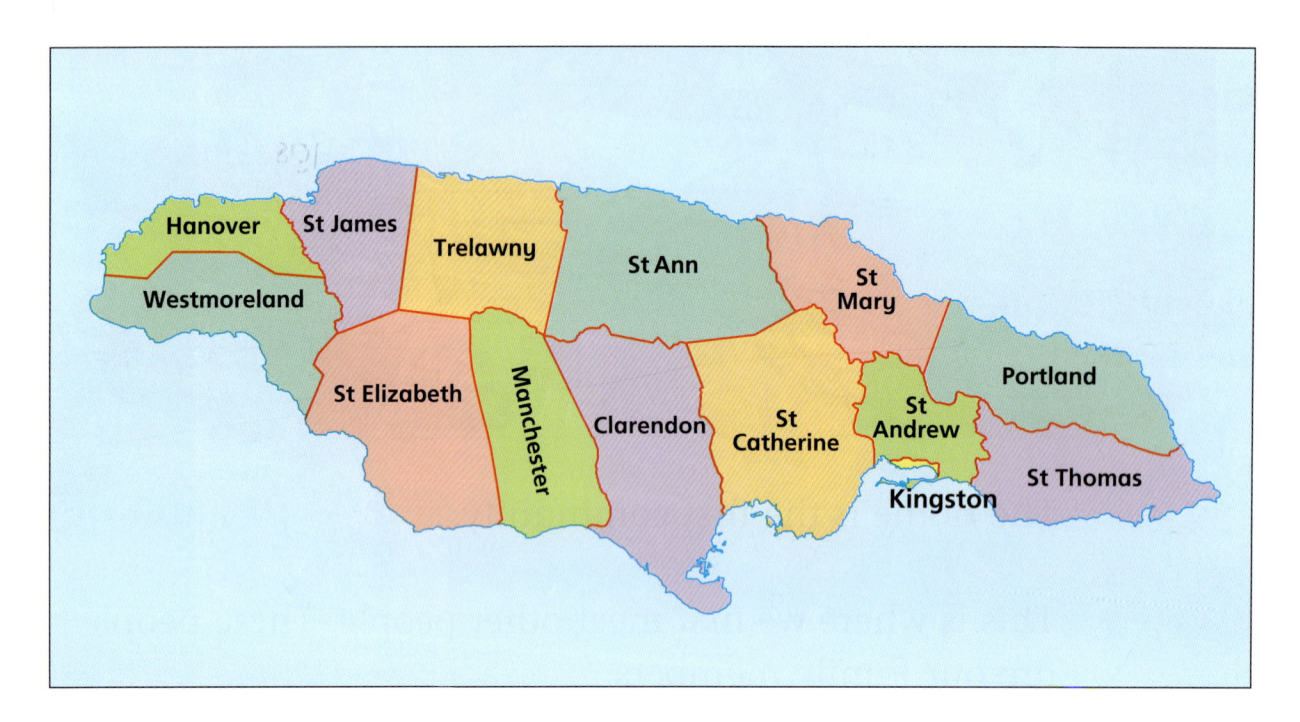

Some communities are in cities.
Others are in the country areas.

- Identify the parish in which you live on the map of Jamaica.
- Say the name of your community.

Relationships in mathematics

In communities, neighbours care for, and share things with, each other.
This helps them to develop good relationships.

There are also relationships in mathematics.
Look at these pictures.

Here we have 12 eggs.
We can also say that we have 1 dozen eggs.
We now know that 12 items make 1 dozen.

If I buy 1 dozen eggs
I get 12 eggs

One dozen = 12

If I buy $\frac{1}{2}$ dozen eggs
I get 6 eggs

Half a dozen = 6

If I buy $\frac{1}{4}$ dozen eggs
I get 3 eggs

Quarter of a dozen = 3

If I buy $\frac{3}{4}$ dozen eggs
I get 9 eggs

Three quarters of a dozen = 9

The 'gh' relationship

Some words are related.

Read this short passage.
Identify the words that are related.
　　At eight o'clock tonight, leave enough cough medicine for Jim.
　　He has had a tough week of illness.
　　He is losing weight and the rough cough is making him weak.

Do you notice that many of the words in the passage share a 'gh' relationship?

Look at how we can use some of these 'gh' words in sentences.

I have eight marbles.

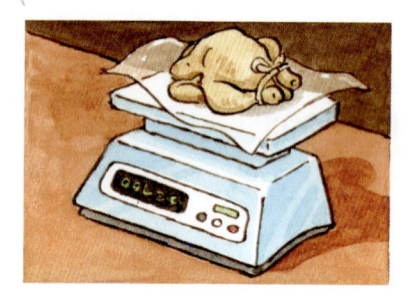

The scale showed the weight of the chicken.

The high waves made the sea rough.

The cough medicine is on the table.

Page 10

Measurements

Did you know that there are ways of measuring almost everything?

Fishermen, farmers and vendors all need to weigh their goods before they are sold.
The goods are weighed to make sure that customers get the correct weight.

A scale is used to measure how heavy things are.

Here are some scales.

A lever arm balance doesn't tell the weight of something; it *compares* the weights of two objects.

The heavier object goes down while the lighter object goes up.
Your teacher will show you how this works.

We measure weight in kilograms or kilos.
Your weight can be measured in kilograms.
Lots of food is packaged in kilograms.

- Look around the kitchen at home.
  How many kilogram packages you can find?

13.2 What's in a name?

Names

Do you know anyone with any of these names? Read them aloud.

Margaret	Ann	Rose	Hope	Clark	Brown
Peter	Maria	Mary	Green	Albert	Catherine
Frank	Hall	Gayle	Thompson		

Would you be surprised to learn that these are the names of some of your communities?

- Read the list of places and where they are found.

Community	Parish
Port Maria	St Mary
St Margaret's Bay	Portland
Rose Hall	St James
Rose Valley	St Catherine
St Ann's Bay	St Ann
Hopewell	Hanover
Frankfield	Clarendon
Thompson Town	Clarendon
Albert Town	Trelawny
Clarks Town	Trelawny
Browns Town	St Ann
Petersfield	Westmoreland
Green Island	Hanover
Gayle	St Mary

Page 13

- Read the list of places again.
- Point to them on this map.

Port Maria	Thompson Town
St Margaret's Bay	Albert Town
Rose Hall	Clarks Town
Rose Valley	Browns Town
St Ann's Bay	Petersfield
Hopewell	Green Island
Frankfield	Gayle

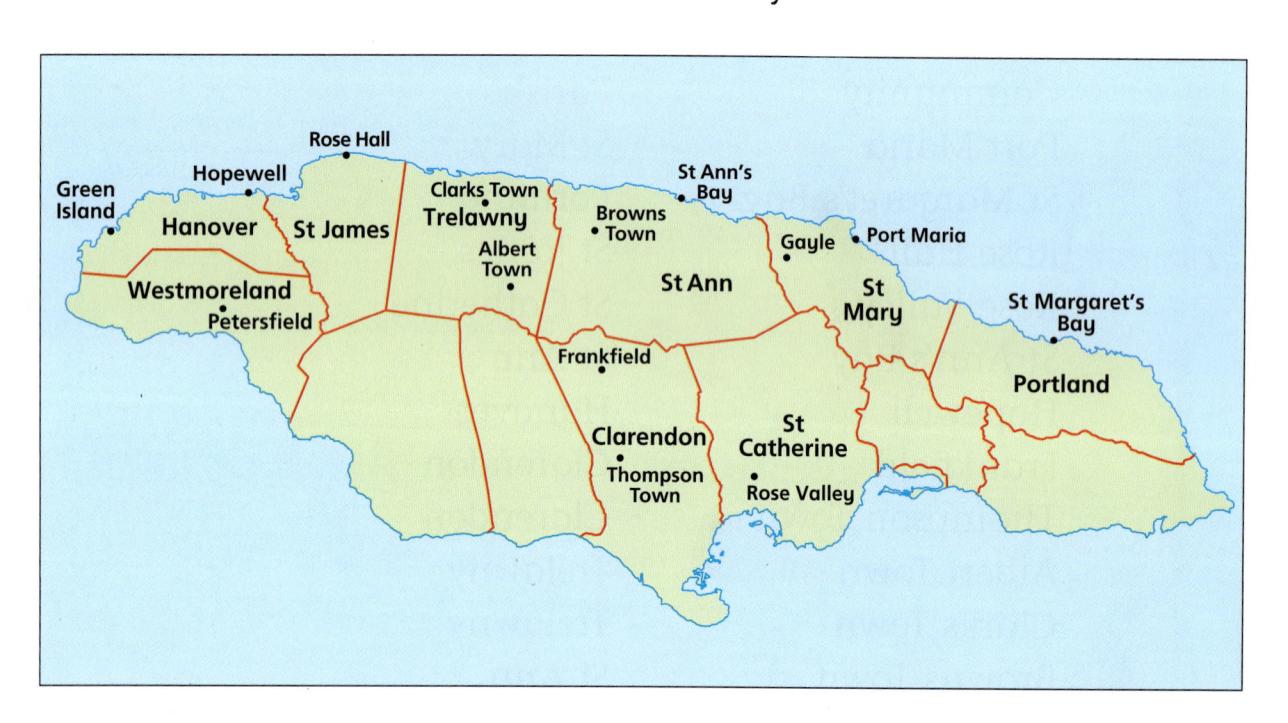

How could you group these names? Talk about this with the class.

Fun as you learn

Tammie, Gordon and Joudy-Ann all have fun learning about other communities.

You too can have fun as you learn about the many communities in Jamaica.

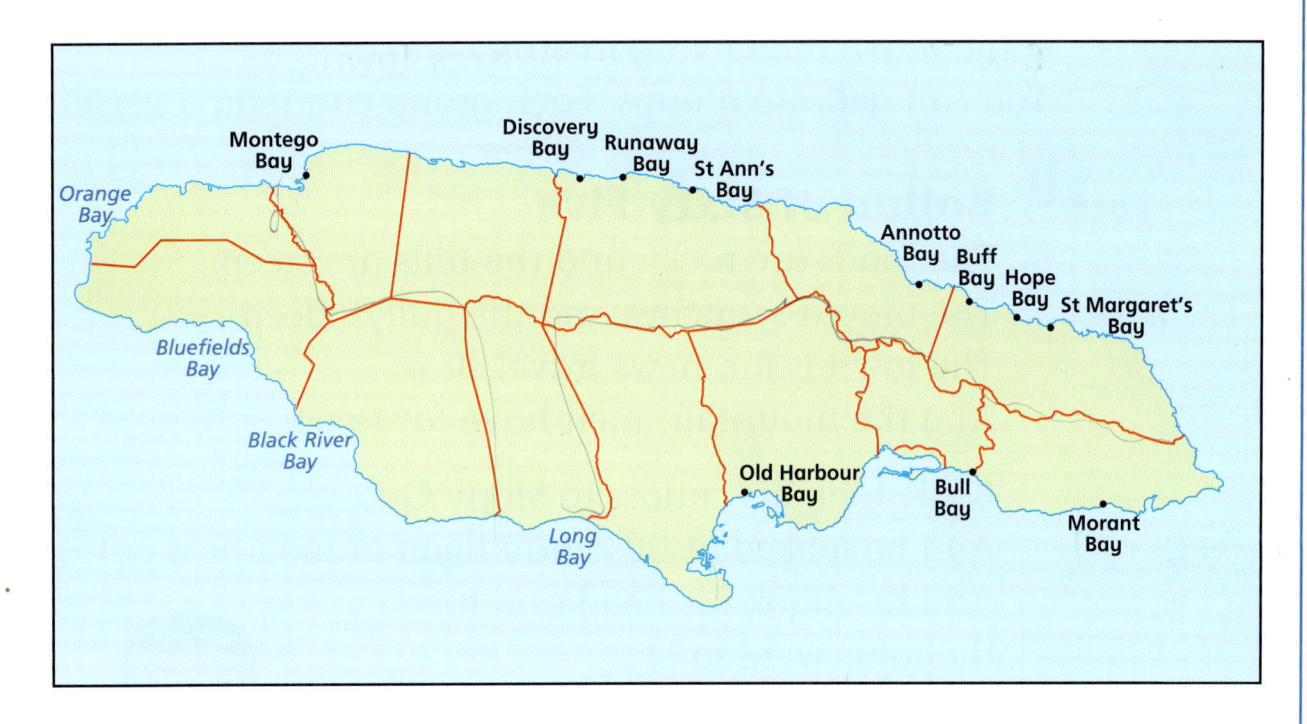

- How many communities are marked on the map?
- What do you notice about where they are located? Are they on the coast or inland?

How are these communities different from inland communities?
Talk about this with the class.

A brave community

Can you say what very sad but important event took place in Morant Bay in the year 1865?

Here are some verses from a poem that will help you to answer.
It is the story of what happened in the year 1865 to some brave men living in Stony Gut.
You can get into groups. Each group can read a verse.

Poem: **Ballad of Sixty-Five**

The roads are rocky and the hills are steep
The macca scratches and the gully's deep
The town is far, news travel slow
And the mountain men have far to go.

Bogle took his cutlass to Stony Gut
And he looked at the small heap of food he'd got
And he shook his head and his thoughts were sad
'You can wuk like a mule but the crop is still bad.'

Bogle got his men and he led them down
Over the hills to Spanish Town
They chopped their way and they made a track
To the Governor's house. But he sent them back.

As they trudged back home to Stony Gut
Paul's spirit sank with each bush he cut
For he thought of the hungry St Thomas men
Who were waiting for the message he'd bring to them.

Then Bogle thundered, 'This thing is wrong
They think we weak, but we hill men strong
Rouse up yourself. We'll march all night
To the Vestry house, and we'll claim our right.'

The Monday morning was tropic clear
As the men from Stony Gut grew near
Clenching their sticks in their farmer's hand
To claim their rights in their native land.

They ran for the bush where they hoped to hide
But the soldiers poured in from Kingston side
They took their prisoners to Morant Bay
Where they hanged them high in the early day.

Paul Bogle died but his spirit talks
Anywhere in Jamaica that freedom walks
Where brave men gathered and courage thrills
As it did those days in St Thomas hills.

Alma Norman

Read the poem again and tell what you think is happening.

Discuss these questions in a group:
- How many lines are in each verse?
- What do you notice about the words at the end of each pair of lines?
- What do you notice about the words Paul Bogle says?

Is the community being described in the poem similar to the community in which you live?

Who do you think Paul Bogle is?
Share what you know about Paul Bogle with your class.

Did you know…?

Some communities in Jamaica have names of communities found in the Bible. Here are the names of some.

> There is a community called **Jericho** in Hanover.
> **Bethlehem** is a community in St Elizabeth.
> **Mount Zion** is a community in the parish of St James.
> **Bethany** is in Manchester.

Say the names of any other communities you know which have names from the Bible.

Here is a song about one community called Jericho. Sing it as a class.

Song: **The Walls of Jericho**
Round the walls of Jericho
Round the walls of Jericho
Round the walls of Jericho
The army marched.
Seven times without a shout
Seven times without a shout
Seven times without a shout
The army marched.
Then the people made a shout
Then the people made a shout
Then the people made a shout
And the walls fell down.

13.3 Using maps

Important buildings in a community

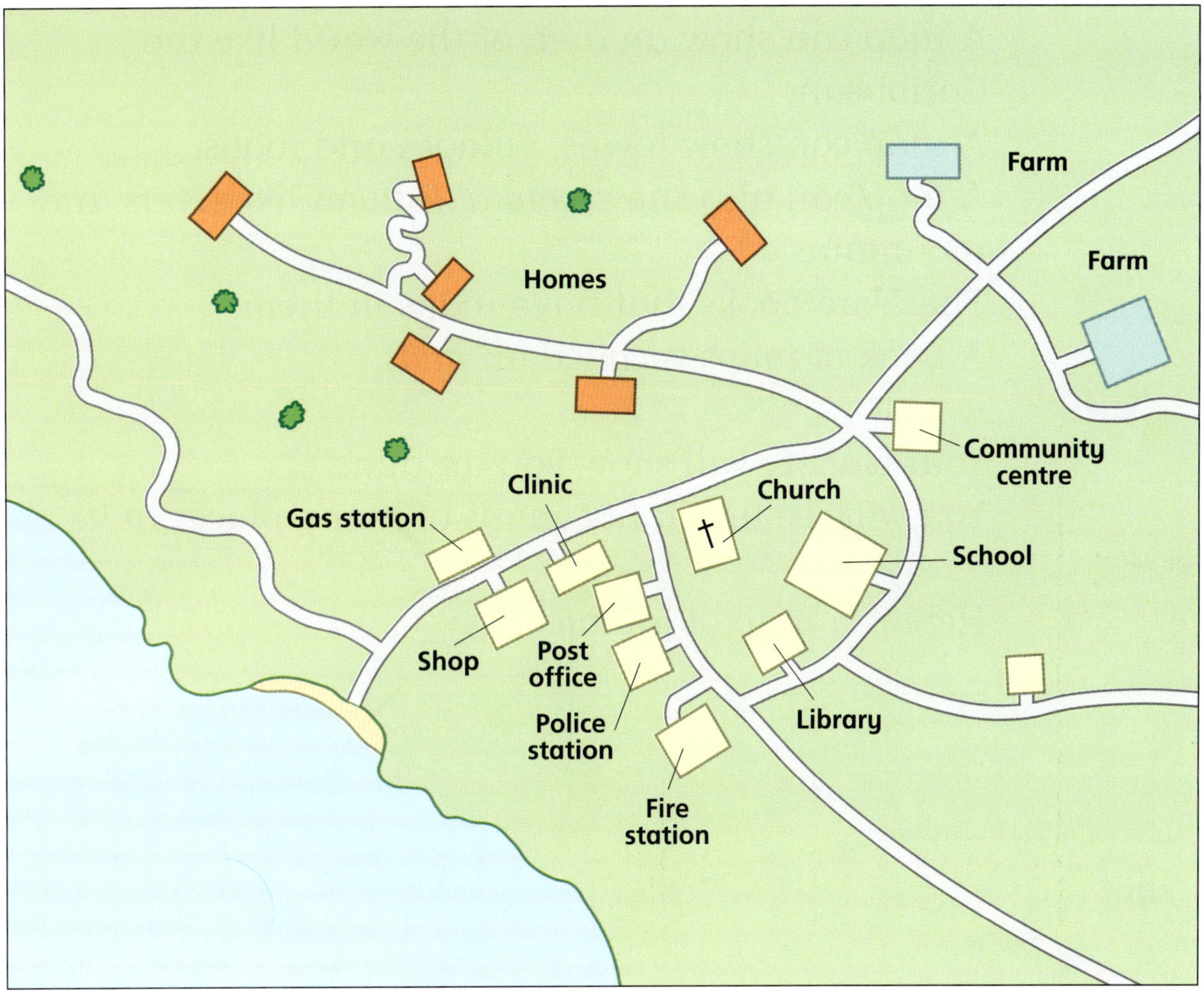

Farm
Farm
Homes
Community centre
Church
Clinic
Gas station
School
Shop
Post office
Police station
Library
Fire station

Here is a drawing of a rural community.
It is a map. A map can show part or all of a community.
It can show where the important buildings are.
It can also show where the homes are and the roads to get from one place to another.

Is this community like your community in any way?
Talk with your teacher and classmates about it.

Jamaica

A map can show part or all of a country.
A map can show an area of the world like the Caribbean.
A map can show towns, villages and roads.
A map can also show *natural features* like rivers and mountains.
There are books that have maps in them.
A book of maps is called an *atlas*.

Your teacher will show you an atlas.
You will see that it has maps of many places in it.

Here is a map of Jamaica.

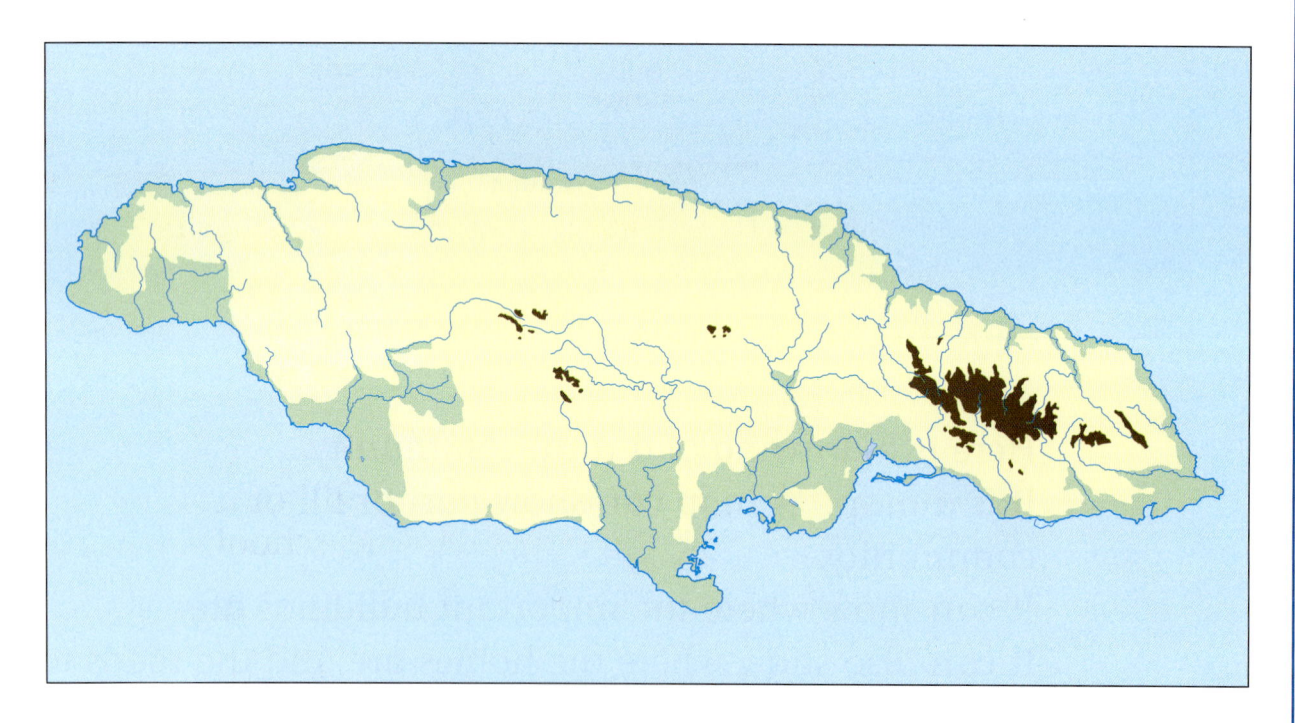

It shows the shape of our island and its rivers, mountains, hills and plains. They are all natural things. Nature provided them.

Look at the map.
The rivers are shown in blue.
The mountains are brown and the hills are shown in yellow.
The plains are shown in green. Plains are also called flat lands.

The capital of Westmoreland is Savanna-la-Mar. It comes from the Spanish word 'savannah' which means flat land or plain.

Tell which plain or very large piece of flat land on the map is in Westmoreland.

There are other communities that have names that tell about the community.

Fruitful Vale in Portland is a fruitful community in a valley. Vale is another word for valley and fruitful means that it grows lots of fruit. This name suits the community.

- Find out how your community got its name.

You can write a letter to an older person in the community inviting them to visit your school to share some interesting information about the community with your class.

- Talk about the things you would want to include in the letter.

Prepositions

Read the sentence about the ladder.

A ladder leans against a tree.

The word 'against' is a *preposition*.
A preposition is a word that shows the relationship between a noun or pronoun and another word in a sentence.
What is the relationship between the ladder and the tree? The ladder is **against** the tree.

Let us look at these pictures.
Read each sentence and identify the *prepositions*.

The mouse is under the chair.

The dog jumped over the fence.

Pam is sitting on the bed.

The cat is sitting beside the door.

13.4 Bible communities

Jesus in the community

In the Bible we read of many communities that Jesus visited while He lived on earth. As He went from one community to another He told the people who had gathered to hear Him about the love of God. He encouraged people to do good to others. We too should try to do the same each day.

This map shows some of the communities that Jesus visited.

- Point to the sea.
- Point to the coastline.
- Point to the rivers and lakes.
- Point to the communities and say their names.

Story: **A Wedding in Cana**

Jesus, His disciples and His mother, Mary, were guests at a wedding at Cana. This was a community in Galilee.

The guests at the wedding were having a good time. Eventually the wine was finished and there was no more to serve the guests. Mary went to Jesus and said 'There is no more wine.' Then she told the attendants, 'Do exactly as He tells you to do.'

Jesus said to the attendants, 'Go and fill some jars with water.'

After they had done this He said to them, 'Take some water from one of the jars and give it to the person in charge of the feast to taste.'

They did this and to their surprise the water had turned to wine.

The attendants told the bridegroom what had happened. Everyone was surprised that this new wine tasted much better than the first. Some people thought it was a plan to keep the best wine until last. This was not so. The truth was that Jesus had performed a miracle by turning water into wine. This was His first miracle on Earth.

After this miracle Jesus and His disciples went on to Capernaum.

- Find Cana and Capernaum on the map on page 23.
- Point to them and read their names.
- Read the names of the other places.

You can read more about this miracle in St John Chapter 2.

Quotation marks

Look again at the story about the wedding in Cana. The exact words spoken by Jesus and Mary have marks that look like commas at the start and the end of the sentences. These are called *quotation marks*.

If we are writing and we want to show the exact words someone said we must remember to use these marks. Printed material often uses single quotation marks 'like this'.
Written material often uses double quotation marks "like this".
If we are just reporting what someone said and not using their exact words we do not need these marks.

Look at these pairs of sentences.

'Please colour the map of Jamaica,' said the teacher.

The teacher told the students to colour the map of Jamaica.

'You must go to the market today,' said my mother.

My mother told us to go to the market today.

> Talk about the difference between these sentences with your teacher.

Page 26

Odds and evens

Quotation marks always appear in pairs. Other things can be placed in pairs.

The fisherman has six fish. The fish are in pairs on the side of his canoe.
We can see that no fish is left by itself. This tells us that the number six is *even*.

The market vendor has seven cabbages. The cabbages are arranged in pairs.
We can see that one cabbage is left by itself. This tells us that the number seven is *odd*.

- Is five an even number or an odd number?

Give a reason for your answer.

Counting by twos

Count up in twos. Here are the numbers you say.

2   4   6   8   10   12   14   16   18   20

These are even numbers.

Count up in twos. Here are the numbers you say.

1   3   5   7   9   11   13   15   17   19

These are odd numbers.

Look at the pattern of even and odd numbers on this grid.

1   2   **3**   4   **5**   6   **7**   8   **9**   10

11 12 **13** 14 **15** 16 **17** 18 **19** 20

21 22 **23** 24 **25** 26 **27** 28 **29** 30

31 32 **33** 34 **35** 36 **37** 38 **39** 40

41 42 **43** 44 **45** 46 **47** 48 **49** 50

13.5 More about my community

Persuasive writing

It can be fun visiting friends and family members in their community.

It can also be fun writing to inform others about the community in which we live.

We could write a letter, a story or an advertisement.

We might try to *persuade* them to visit our community. When you persuade someone you try to get him or her to act in a certain way.
On the next two pages we are going to look at a persuasive letter and a persuasive advertisement.

Happy Grove
St Elizabeth
June 25th 2006

Dear Tammie
I learned a lot about your community from your letter. I would like to tell about where I live and invite you to visit my family and me. It would be as we swim and splash and dive in the clear water of the Caribbean S
My uncle is a fisherman and so I could ask him to treat us to a ride i canoe. My father fries lovely festival and fish so I will ask him to cook some for us.
We can also take a bus to Boston because it is not very far from where live. In Boston there is very nice jerk pork and chicken. This is lovely wi roasted breadfruit. There is a lovely beach there so we could even have picnic too.
Going to the Nonsuch Caves would also be fun. I hope you will not be a because inside the caves it is dark. Another fun place to go would be R Falls. I go there because it is not very far from my home. I am also tryi be very good because my big plan is to ask mom and dad to take us raf on the Rio Grande. Do you know that Rio Grande are Spanish words tha mean Great River?
I hope you will get to visit me because we do have a lot of fun in the communities too.

Your friend

Joudy-Ann

A letter

Visit Falmouth
see the historic buildings and Hampden Wharf
or you could hop to nearby Montego Bay to enjoy many water sports
at the end of the day relax as you raft on the peaceful Martha Brae.
Talk with friends and natives and learn about Trelawney! Take a trip to the market to buy fine produce and craft items for your home.

An advertisement

Page 29

A persuasive letter

Happy Grove
St Elizabeth
June 25th 2006

Dear Tammie

I learned a lot about your community from your letter. I would like to tell you about where I live and invite you to visit my family and me. It would be fun as we swim and splash and dive in the clear water of the Caribbean Sea.

My uncle is a fisherman and so I could ask him to treat us to a ride in his canoe. My father fries lovely festival and fish so I will ask him to cook some for us.

We can also take a bus to Boston because it is not very far from where I live. In Boston there is very nice jerk pork and chicken. This is lovely with roasted breadfruit. There is a lovely beach there so we could even have a picnic too.

Going to the Nonsuch Caves would also be fun. I hope you will not be afraid because inside the caves it is dark. Another fun place to go would be Reach Falls. I go there because it is not very far from my home. I am also trying to be very good because my big plan is to ask mom and dad to take us rafting on the Rio Grande. Do you know that Rio Grande are Spanish words that mean Great River?

I hope you will get to visit me because we do have a lot of fun in the rural communities too.

Your friend

Joudy-Ann

Tammie may visit Joudy-Ann because of the letter she wrote.

Tammie learnt about Joudy-Ann's community and some neighbouring ones.

Page 30

A persuasive advertisement

Look at this advertisement. Read it and talk about what you have learnt with your classmates.

Visit Falmouth
See the historic buildings and Hampden Wharf.
or you could hop to nearby Montego Bay to enjoy many water sports.
at the end of the day relax as you raft on the peaceful Martha Brae.
Talk with friends and natives and learn about Trelawney! Take a trip to the market to buy fine produce and craft items for your home.

From this advertisement we learn that:
- Falmouth is in Trelawny.
- The Hampden Wharf is in Falmouth.
- Montego Bay is not very far from Falmouth.
- Rafting takes place on the Martha Brae River, which is in Trelawny.
- Falmouth has some historic buildings.
- The people of Falmouth are friendly.

The advertisement makes people want to go to Falmouth.

Pronouns

This is Tammie. Tammie lives in an urban area. Tammie loves writing to Gordon. Gordon lives near the sea.

This is Tammie. She lives in an urban area. She loves writing to Gordon. He lives near the sea.

What was different about the second set of sentences? Did you see that Tammie's name was used once and Gordon's name was used once? The words we used instead of their names are 'she' and 'he'.

Words that are used in place of nouns are called *pronouns*.

Read these two sentences.
   The bird has broken its wing so the bird cannot fly.
   The bird has broken its wing so it cannot fly.

- Which noun has been replaced by 'it' in the second sentence?

Read these two sentences.
   Mr Johns likes animals and there are lots of pigs, goats and sheep on his farm.
   Mr Johns likes animals and there are lots of them on his farm.

- Which nouns have been replaced by the word 'them' in the second sentence?

Roman numerals

The numbers we normally use are called *Arabic* numerals.

On the faces of some clocks we see a different kind called *Roman* numerals. These are the numerals that were used by the ancient Romans.

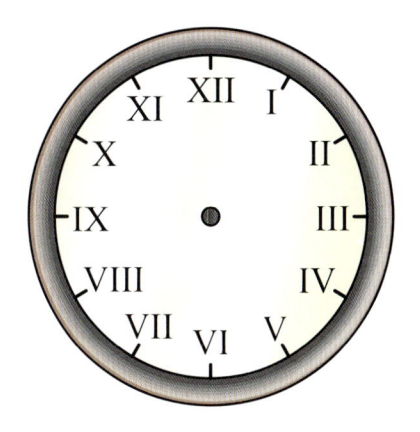

Here are the numbers from one to twelve in Arabic and Roman numerals.

Arabic numerals	Roman numerals
1	I
2	II
3	III
4	IIII or IV
5	V
6	VI
7	VII
8	VIII
9	VIIII or IX
10	X
11	XI
12	XII

- What do you think the Roman numeral for 13 is?

- What is the time on this clock?

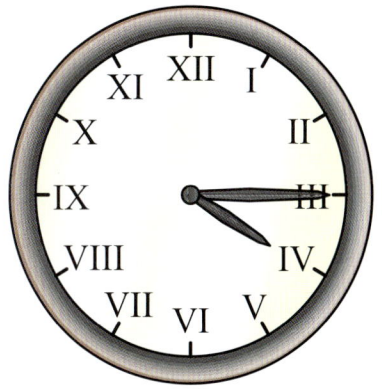

Page 33

14 What does my community look like?

14.1 Buildings in the community

What's in a building?

Important buildings in communities can be put into groups in different ways.

They can be put into groups according to their age, their shape and size and the materials used to make them.

Some buildings that are over one hundred years old are protected by the *National Heritage Trust*. This is because they are of historical importance to the Nation.

Here are some buildings that are protected by the National Heritage Trust.

St Joseph's Teachers' College, Kingston

Rose Hall Great House, Montego Bay

Shapes of buildings

Shape and size can be used to classify important buildings in a community.

Most important buildings are large.

The shapes of churches tell the denomination of the people who worship in them.

Anglican church   Methodist church    Catholic church

Building materials

Older buildings are built with bricks, wood and shingle. Their windows are generally made of wooden lattice work and their doors and floors are of hardwood.

An old building

A modern building

Modern buildings are often built with concrete.

The walls are made with block and steel, windows are made using wood and glass or metal and glass. Floors are made of wood, terrazzo or ceramic tiles and doors are wooden, metal or glass.

Comparisons

Some buildings are built with wood and stone.
These are *natural* building materials.

Other buildings are built with concrete and bricks.
These are *man-made* building materials.

- Compare the old building and the modern building in the photographs on page 36. Discuss them with the person sitting next to you. What similarities and what differences can you see?

Here are some words we use to compare things, animals and people.

Big fish

Bigger fish

Biggest fish

Heavy book

Heavier book

Heaviest book

- Make some comparing words from 'tall'. Say a sentence with each word in it.

Page 37

Small words hidden inside bigger words

The word 'community' has nine letters.

Read and talk about the smaller words that are hidden inside it.

i	1 letter
it	2 letters
nit	3 letters
unit	4 letters
unity	5 letters
mutiny	6 letters

- Find some smaller words hidden in the word 'England'.

Opposites

Read these sentences.

Kerry-Ann lives inland in an old house in a rural community.

Bryan lives on the coast in a modern house in the city, in an urban community.

Say some pairs of words from these sentences that mean the opposite of each other.

Here they are:

inland is the opposite of **coast**
old is the opposite of **modern**
country is the opposite of **city**
rural is the opposite of **urban**

Look at the pictures and read these opposite words with a friend.

flood

drought

masculine

feminine

generous

mean

- Now start with the first pair of opposites and make up a pair of sentences using one of the words in each.
- Do the same for the other opposite pairs.

14.2 Natural features of the community

Weather changes in the community

Weather tells us of the changes in the atmosphere.

Here are some words we use to describe the weather.

windy   cloudy   sunny   rainy
foggy   overcast   fair   changeable

This pictograph shows what the weather was like for one week in Fruitful Vale.

Sunday	Monday	Tuesday	Wednesday	Thursday	Friday	Saturday

Here is some information that the pictograph gives us.

Three days were rainy: Monday, Thursday and Saturday
Two days were sunny: Tuesday and Wednesday
One day was cloudy: Sunday
One day was overcast: Friday

- On which days do you think the farmers would be working in their fields?
- On which days do you think they would not?

The farmers would probably be working in their fields on the days when it was not raining. We have come to a *conclusion* based on what we know about how farmers work.

We often come to *conclusions*. Read these conclusions and discuss them with your classmates.

If you study hard at school we conclude that you will get good grades.

If you eat lots of fruits and vegetables we conclude that you will stay healthy.

If you look both ways before crossing the street we conclude that you will cross safely.

If you walk or cycle everywhere we conclude that your muscles will become strong and fit.

> Share some more conclusions with the class.

Phonics 'ph' sound

Two letters can go together to give one sound.

When the letters 'ph' are written together they give the sound of a letter 'f'.

Say these words out loud. Listen for the 'f' sound.

atmosphere   pictograph   graph

Here are some more words containing 'ph'.

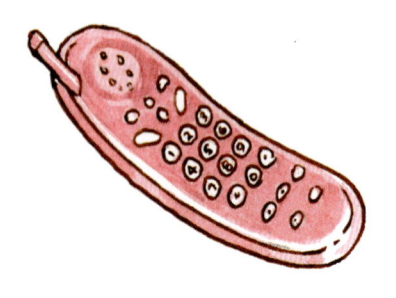

telephone

Pharisee

dolphin

elephant

alphabet

typhoon

photograph

phantom

pharmacy

Some people have names containing the 'ph' sound.
Read these names out loud.

Philip   **Philippa**   **Josephine**   **Joseph**

Think of some other 'ph' words. Share them with your class.

Page 42

Forming plurals by adding 'es'

Some nouns form their plural by adding '-es' to the base word. Here are some examples.

One — More than one

glass — glasses

brush — brushes

bench — benches

When a noun ends in s, x or ch we add '-es' to make it plural.

> Think of a word that ends with each of these letters. Say the singular word and then the plural word.

15　Who are the people in my community?

15.1 The same but different

Census

A *census* is a count of people who live in a country at a given time.

A population census is done every five years.
During census time, only people who are eighteen years old or older are interviewed by the census taker.

Census takers ask people questions about themselves and their families.

Here are some of the things they ask people about.

age   **sex/gender**   **marital status**   **siblings**
birth place   **occupation**   **education**
ethnic group   **religion**

Here is a dictionary of census words:

Word	This means…
age	how old you are
birthplace	the district, parish or town in which you were born
education	where you went to school and/or college and what public examinations you have passed
ethnic group	your nationality of origin, for example Chinese, Indian
marital status	whether you are married or single
occupation	the kind of work you do
religion	the church you attend and who is regarded as the Supreme Being
sex/gender	whether you are male or female
siblings	your brothers and sisters

A census can also be taken at school, at church or at the work place.
This helps to find out the number of people at each place at a given time.

A class census

A census is a count of people who are at a certain place at a given time. A census could be taken of the denominations in a class.

The denominations of the students in a class are 10 Baptists, 8 Anglicans, 6 Jehovah's Witness, 9 Pentecostals and 5 Seventh Day Adventists.

The information can be displayed as a bar graph.

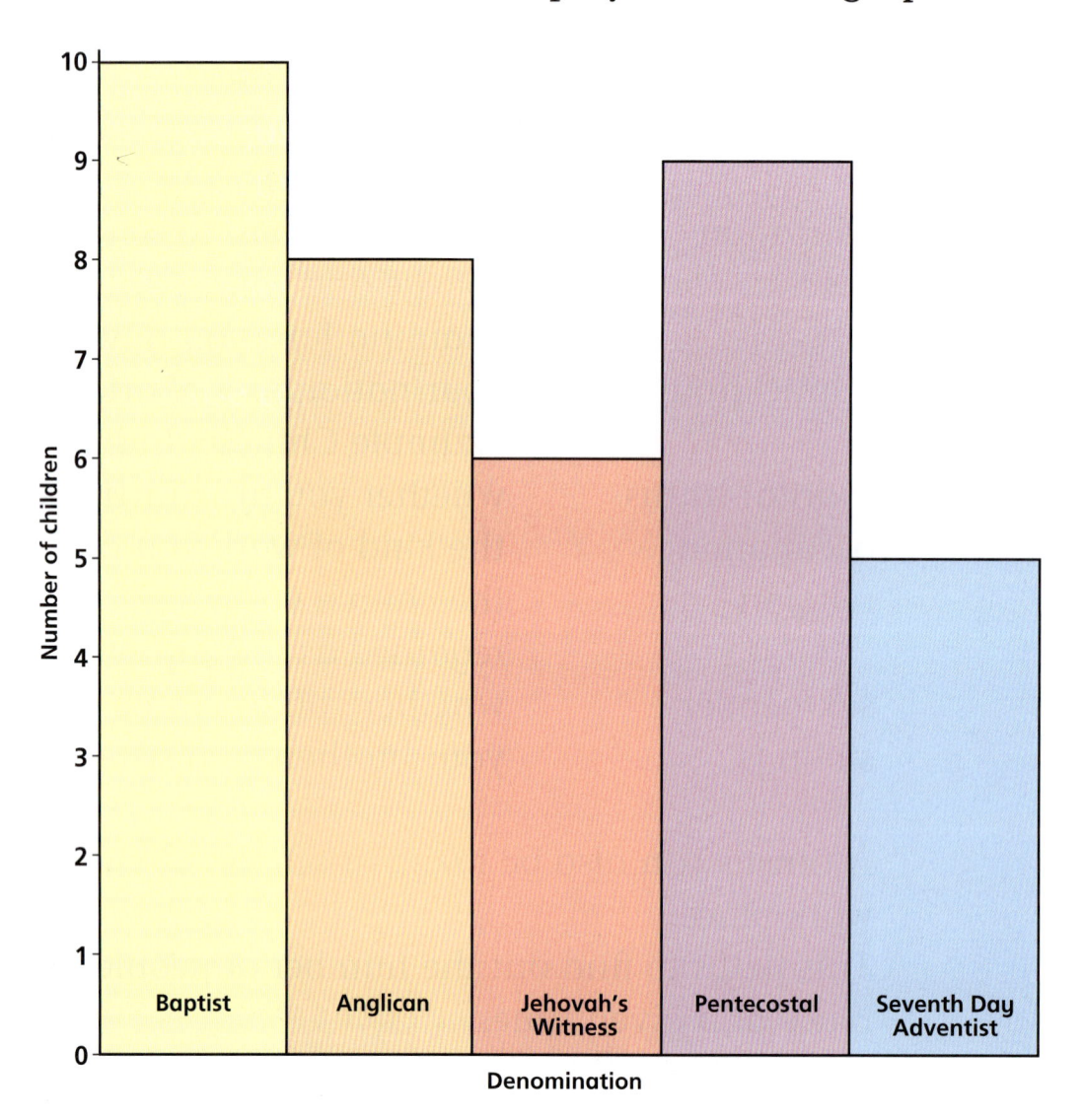

Work for me and see

Story: **Anancy and the Magic Pot**

Anancy was well known for his lazy ways. Instead of working to take care of his family, he would spend many hours thinking about ways to trick others and get some of the nice things they had.

One day Anancy and his family had nothing to eat so he left home to search for food. As he walked through the bushes he saw an old pot. He looked at the pot and said, 'What is an old pot doing here?' To his surprise the pot said,'I am not an old pot. My name is work for me and see.'

Anancy was shocked but he managed to say, 'Work for me and see?' He did not know that it was a magic pot and so he was even more shocked when the pot cooked a lovely meal. Anancy, however, was not too surprised to be able eat the food all by himself. 'This is the best day of my life. I will never have to work again,' he said to himself, 'and my family will never be hungry again.'

'I must take this pot home,' he said out loud.
'Take me home,' said the pot, 'but be sure not to wash me. If you do, I will never be able to cook you food again.'
'My wife is a very clean woman. If she sees the pot she will certainly wash it. I must hide it from her,' said Anancy to himself.

So, Anancy hid the pot in a secret place in a room of his home. Each day at a certain time he would go to the room when no one was looking and say 'work for me and see,' and the pot would cook anything Anancy asked for. Then he would share the food with his family.

Can you imagine how fat and lazy Anancy became? All he did was eat and sleep. His wife kept asking him where he got such nice food from and he would say things like 'Brenda Tiger and Mary Monkey helped me out, my wife.' His wife did not believe this story and so she began to watch him, and one day she found out the trick.

One morning when her husband was out she went to the room, took out the pot and said, 'Work for me and see.' Very soon the pot cooked a lovely stew. She fed the children and what do you think she did? She washed the pot and put it back in its place so her husband would not find out.

That day Anancy was out visiting friends. When he came home he went straight to the room and said the magic words to the pot. To his surprise he got no food. He was very upset when he found out he would get no more food and, worst of all, he would have to work if he wanted to eat. He tossed the pot straight through the window.

His wife tried to comfort him but all Anancy could think of was why his wife had to be so clean.

'Jack mandora mi no choose non.'

> Do you think Anancy was wrong to be so lazy?
> Do you think his wife was wrong to use the pot without asking permission?
> Discuss the story with your class.

Page 49

15.2 Comparing individuals

Opposites

Read this poem.

Poem: **Neighbours**
The people who live on the right of us
Are very quiet and make no fuss,
But the family on the left clatter about
Day and night, and sometimes shout.
Yet the people on the left of us
Are really rather marvellous
Instead of being put out by everything
They burst out laughing and sing.
But the family who live on the right of us
Often make me curious
The way the father whispers to the mother,
The sister and her silent brother.
I suppose that neighbours are meant
To be different.

Leonard Clarke

When we compare people or things we can look at their similarities and differences.

In the poem 'Neighbours', some of the people were quiet while others made a clatter.
The noisy neighbours were often about, day and night.
One set of neighbours lived on the right and the other lived on the left.

The words: **quiet** and **clatter**
day and **night**
right and **left** are opposites of each other.

More about opposites

Look at the sets of pictures and call the words.

Page 51

Comparing numbers

We use the signs > and < to compare numbers.

Remember that the sign > means 'greater than' and the sign < means 'less than'.

It is convenient to use these signs to compare numbers.

Read these word sentences and number sentences.

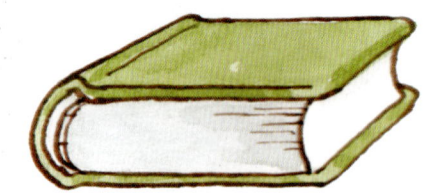

I have two books. One book has 132 pages. The other has 96 pages.

I can use a number sentence to compare the books.
132 pages > 96 pages

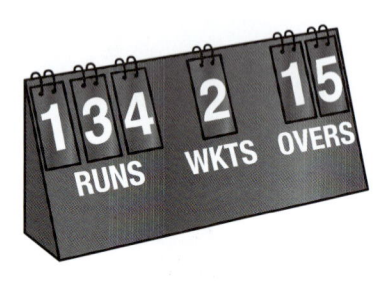

In a cricket match one team scored 134 runs.
The other scored 186 runs.

I can use a number sentence to compare the scores.
134 runs < 186 runs

Page 52

Groups in a community

In a community people gather together for different reasons.
They gather together at church, for games and sports, for funerals, to demonstrate, to work or to give concerts.

We give the people gathered together different names based on what they are doing.

These people are at a church so we call them a **congregation**.

Here are the **staff** who work in an office.

Children at school are called pupils or **students**.

Here is a **crowd** of people holding a demonstration.

Two **teams** are playing basketball.

The **audience** is enjoying the concert.

The **mourners** at the funeral are very sad.

The **regiment** of soldiers looks smart in uniform.

My **neighbours** are very helpful.

The ship's **crew** sail the boat well.

Try to remember these group names and use them correctly when you speak or write.

Animal groups

Animals also have group names.

A **flock** of birds.

A **swarm** of bees.

A **herd** of cows.

A **shoal** of fish.

A **brood** of chicks.

A **litter** of puppies

An **army** of ants

A **pride** of lions.

A **school** of dolphins.

Page 55

All about gender

We can group things that are alike together.
For instance we can group things together by *gender*.

We have *masculine* gender, *feminine* gender and *neuter* gender.

Look at these groups and their gender.

**These are all males so their gender is *masculine*.
Mr, he, his and him are words that describe masculine gender.**

**These are all females so their gender is *femimine*.
Mrs, Miss, she and her are words that describe feminine gender.**

Some words are neither masculine nor feminine so we say they are the *neuter* gender.
If there are no pictures we cannot tell whether a neuter word applies to a male or a female.

Here are some examples of neuter words. Read them out.

animal   baby   teacher   parent   person   child

15.3 Comparing communities

Different kinds of communities

Tammie's community is Meadowbrook and it is in Kingston.
Kingston is a city so it is an *urban* community.
There are no shops, markets or supermarkets in Tammie's community.
We can also call Meadowcroft a *residential* community.
It is a group of houses where people live but they don't work there as well.

Joudy-Ann's community is in St Elizabeth and it is not in a town.
It is in a country area so we call it a *rural* community.

In Joudy-Ann's community many people live and work on farms.
We can also call it a *farming* community.

Gordon's community is near to the sea.
Some of the men work there as fishermen while the women are fish vendors. They sell fish to people on the beach.
Gordon lives in a *fishing* community.
Some of the people who live there work outside the fishing community. They do other jobs like building, domestic help, teaching, preaching and office work.

Now you know about the communities of these three children.

- Are their communities like yours in any way? Talk with your teacher about this.

Get into groups and discuss your community.
Write your ideas down in your journals and illustrate them.

More about rural and urban communities

Poem: **Community**

We all belong to a community.
And we are expected to live in unity.
Some communities are very small
With people who are short or tall.

There are communities that are very large
To move around on a bus there is a charge.
There are many buildings for us to see
And the people work together like busy bees.

Heidi Johnson

Districts and villages are called rural communities. They are small communities.

Towns and cities are called urban communities. They are large communities.

Kingston and Montego Bay are urban communities. Here are some differences between rural communities and urban communities.

Rural communities	Urban communities
Few people.	Many people.
May not have electricity or piped water.	Have electricity and piped water.
No telephone service.	Telephone service.
Small grocery shops and stores.	Large supermarkets and shopping centres.
Buildings may be far apart.	Buildings are close together.
Mostly farm vehicles.	Many different vehicles.
Few business places.	Many business places.
Postal Agency.	Post Office.
Few primary and secondary schools.	Many schools including colleges and universities.

Comparisons using 'as'

We can compare things by using the word 'as'. Look at the pictures and read the sentences. Discuss them with your teacher.

Maria and Tamieka are <u>as</u> playful <u>as</u> puppies.

Puppies love to play. These two friends also love to play. In this way they act like puppies and so we compare them to puppies.

Debon runs <u>as</u> fast <u>as</u> lightning.

Lightning moves very quickly across the sky. Debon moves very quickly when he runs so we compare him with lightning.

Read these comparisons.

As stubborn as a mule.
As proud as a peacock.
As gentle as a lamb.
As sweet as honey.

As happy as a lark.
As frisky as a lamb.
As cold as ice.
As good as gold.

Talk about these comparisons with your teacher.

> More about comparisons

Read this story in a group.

Story: **Sports Day at Lucky Hill**

All the students at Lucky Hill Primary School were excited. They were as happy as larks. It was sports day and all the best runners were on the field.

All the spectators were given drinks that were as sweet as honey and as cold as ice. The spectators were as frisky as lambs. They sang songs and cheered the runners who ran as fast as lightning down the track.

At the end of the day the headmaster said that all of the students had behaved very well and had been as good as gold. The students liked this compliment and were as proud as peacocks.

- How many comparisons were made in the story?

15.4 Workers in the community

Community workers

People are the most important resource in a community.

This means that nothing is more important than the people in the community.

What people in a community do for a living is called *work*.
Work needs effort and energy.
People work to make or produce *goods*.
People also work to provide a *service*.
A service is what someone does for you.

A community cannot function without people. It is the people who provide goods and services.

A carpenter makes goods for people to buy.

A taxi driver provides people with a service.

People are paid for the goods they make or the services they provide.
They use the money to provide themselves and their families with things like food, clothing and shelter.

Community volunteers

Some people *volunteer* their services to help others in the community.
Volunteers are not paid for their services.
Some Red Cross workers are volunteers.

Is there a Red Cross club at your school? If there is one find out what they do. Write the information in your journal. If there isn't one perhaps you and some friends could start one. Ask your teacher for help and advice.

Some people volunteer to help in homes for the elderly and for children.
Do you know the names of any of these homes? Have you ever visited one?

Some ODPEM workers are volunteers.
Did you know that ODPEM is short for:

Office of Disaster Preparedness and Emergency Management

- Can you see where the letters ODPEM come from? Your teacher will help you.

Food for the community

Shopkeepers supply us with food using supermarkets, grocery shops and markets.

Mr George Martin is a farmer.
He has a large farm in the country.
On his farm he grows different kinds of food plants.
He grows yam and sweet potato.
He also grows vegetables such as tomatoes, carrots, cabbage and lettuce.

Most of Mr Martin's foods are sold in the market.
At the market the vendors sell us *ground provisions*, fruits and fresh vegetables.
The ground provisions include yam, sweet potatoes, coco and dasheen.

Mr George Martin also has some chicken coops, with hundreds of chickens.
Some of the chickens lay eggs.
Many of these eggs are sold in the community.
When the other chickens are ready to eat, a big truck collects them and takes them to the broilers.
We buy chickens to eat in the supermarket.
We can also buy meat from the butcher in the market.

The butcher sells different kinds of meat.
The meat he sells includes beef, pork and mutton.

More about food for the community

Other members of the community also provide us with food.

Mother buys fish from Mrs Roach. She pushes a cart.
Mother says that she likes to buy the fish from Mrs Roach because they are always fresh.

At the school gate Miss Little
sells fruits.
We get our apples, ripe bananas
and oranges from her.

The people in the community
support one another.
That is why we are so successful.

Shelter for the community

Some people own their homes. Other people rent the houses in which they live.
It is hard work to build a house. Many people are employed to do the job.
They must work together as a team to build the house or it will not be done properly.

- Name some of these building workers.

Clothing for the community

Our parents buy ready-made clothes from the stores.
They can also buy the material and pay the dressmaker and the tailor in the community to sew them.

Our educational needs

Although our parents and other members of the community supply our basic needs, there are people who supply our other needs.

Our teachers and librarians help us satisfy our educational needs.
Teachers help us to read and write and do mathematics.
Some teachers also help us to keep fit.

Our health needs

The doctor and the nurse provide health care for the community.
Some doctors have private offices, while others work in the clinics and hospitals.
The nurses also work in the clinics and hospitals.
Some of them are dental nurses and they take care of our teeth.

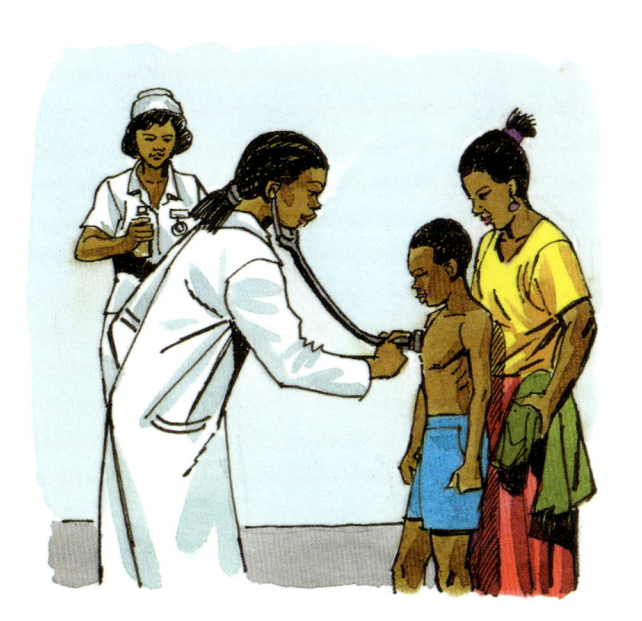

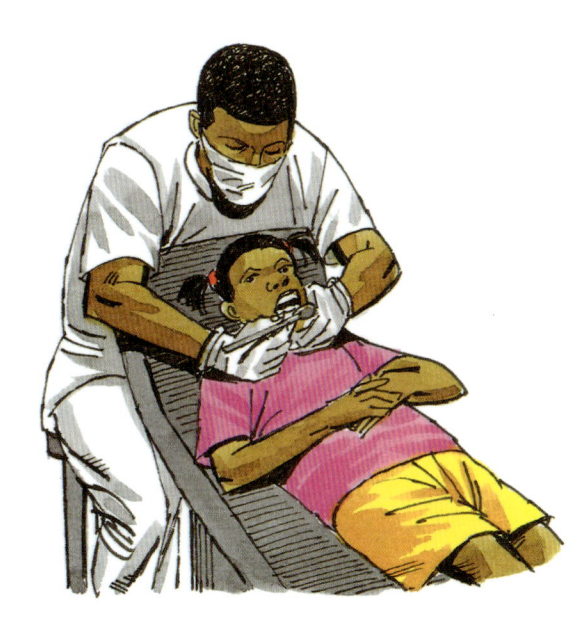

Our spiritual needs

When we go to church, we can say that the preacher is helping us to take care of our spiritual needs.

There are many different kinds of churches and religious groups in our community.

Those who protect us

There are many people in the community who protect us.
They are the police, the firemen and the soldiers.

When we go to the beach, lifeguards protect us.

Talk about how these people protect you.

15.5 Changing times

How times have changed!

Children grow and change.

Plants grow and change.

In communities many things have changed over time. Older family members and people in the community can tell you about some of the changes.

Look at the pictures and discuss them.

- Point to the pictures that tell of long ago. Why did you decide on these pictures?
- Point to the pictures that tell of what is happening today.

Page 72

Today men and women are often doing the same kind of work.
Many farmers are now using machines to plough their lands.
Fewer people use the Post Office because they now have telephones and computers with Internet service.

> If you use a computer, talk about what you use it for.

Are communities new?

You are likely to answer no and that is correct.
People have lived in communities since ancient times.

They did not have any of the modern things that we have now but they worked, cared for their families, worshipped and found time to relax.
They did these things a little differently from the way we do now.

For example, they did not have tractors and metal spades and forks when they farmed the land. They used sharpened sticks, and pointed stones to help them break up the soil.
They could only farm small areas.

Look at this picture of farmers in an ancient community.

- Talk about what you see.
  Are you surprised? Explain if you are surprised or not.

In some modern communities the farms are large.

This is an example of what a modern farmer does if he has a lot of land to cultivate.

In some modern communities the farms are small. The method of farming a small farm is different to that of a large farm.

This is an example of what a modern farmer does if he has a small amount of land to cultivate.

Look again at the pictures.
- Have you ever seen any of the things in the pictures. If so, where did you see them?
- If you have never seen any of these things, why do you think this is so?

An interesting community

Page 75

After slavery came to an end many people came to work on the sugar cane plantations and to do other jobs. These people included East Indians, Chinese, Syrians and Jews.

Descendants of these people live in communities in many parts of Jamaica.
People of these races and cultures help to give Jamaica her rich heritage and culture.
That is why our motto is 'Out of Many, One People'.
The island is one big community.

It does not matter that we look different.
We are all Jamaicans and we should love and respect one another.

Jesus visits another community

Many people who lived on earth during the time of Jesus had jobs similar to the jobs people do now.
For example, some were tax collectors, judges, rabbis or teachers, priests, fishermen, labourers and carpenters. Here is a story about a tax collector Jesus met as He travelled to the community in Jericho.

Story: **Jesus and Zacchaeus**

Once, Jesus visited the community of Jericho. Many people wanted to see Him because they had heard a lot about the many good things that He had done.

Among the persons who had gathered was a tax collector named Zacchaeus. He was very rich and many people thought he collected more tax than was necessary from them. So Zacchaeus was not well liked.
In trying to see the Saviour, Zacchaeus had a problem. He was unable to see Jesus because the crowd was very big and he was too short to see over their heads. However, he had a brilliant idea. He decided to climb a sycamore tree so that he would have a good view.

As soon as Jesus got to where Zacchaeus was He looked up at the tree and said 'Hurry down Zacchaeus because I must stay in your house today.' He hurried down from the tree feeling very happy, but the people were not happy for him. They were all upset to learn that Jesus would be going to the house of a person they thought was evil.

'This man has gone as a guest to the home of a sinner,' the people mumbled.

Zacchaeus felt very sorry for what he had done, so he promised Jesus he would give some of the things he owned to the poor. He also promised to give back to those he had cheated four times as much as he had taken from them.

Jesus forgave him as He said to him, 'Salvation has come to this house today.'

Read more about this visit in the Bible in Luke 19:1–19.

Here is a song about Zacchaeus.

Song:

Zacchaeus was a wee little man
A wee little man was he
He climbed up in a sycamore tree
For the Lord he wanted to see
And as the Saviour passed that way
He looked up in the tree, and He said
'Zacchaeus, you come down, for I am going to your house today.'

Test your acting skills. Get into groups and dramatise the meeting of Jesus and Zacchaeus.

Fun time in the community

Long ago many people did not have electric light in their communities so they could not watch television or do anything that needed electricity. Many adults and children amused themselves by telling stories, jokes and riddles.

Riddles usually start with the words 'riddle mi dis, riddle mi dat, guess me dis riddle and perhaps not'.

This lady is the Honourable Louise Bennett-Coverley.

Many people call the Honourable Louise Bennet-Coverly 'Miss Lou}.

She told many stories, jokes and riddles to Jamaicans.

She also performed in many pantomimes.

Here are a few riddles for you.

Can you guess their answers?

- Sweet water standing up.
- Hell a top, hell a bottom, hallelujah in the middle.
- My father has some children and they all have one eye.
- Why is a river so rich?
- What goes up and never comes down?
- Up chin cheerie, down chin cheerie, no man dear climbs chin cheerie.
- What goes up when the rain comes down?
- Why are Saturday and Sunday strong days?

Check the answers in your Workbook.

15.6 Money

Is money important?

When people work they provide goods or a service for which they get paid.
Their pay is money.
The money they earn is used to pay for goods and services that they need.

Most people put away some of the money they earn.
They join banks, so they can save for their future and to take care of emergencies.

At the beginning of every school year, our parents use some of the money they save to buy school uniform, books and other things that we may need at school.

Our parents must also pay different kinds of taxes.
They pay these taxes because the government needs the money to run the country.
Taxes are paid at the tax office, which is one of the important buildings in our community.

People who own cars, buses, trucks and motorbikes pay taxes too.
They must pay to use their vehicles on the road.

Taxes are also paid on land and on the items that we buy in shops and supermarkets.

We all pay the General Consumption Tax. This is the tax we call GCT.

Money is very important to both the government and the private citizen.
Without money it would be hard to survive.

Getting change

Sometimes when we buy goods we don't have exactly the right money.
We hand in a larger amount and we get some money back.
This money is called change.

We know how much change we get by subtracting the value of the goods from the amount of money we have handed over.
Here are two examples of change.

The cost of two patties was $40.00. I gave the shopkeeper $50.00.

$50.00 − $40.00 = $10.00   or

$	c
50	00
− 40	00
= 10	00

So my change is $10.00.

Page 83

I bought a cake for $15.00 and a bag juice for $10.00. I gave the shopkeeper $30.00.

$30.00 − $15.00 − $10.00 = $5.00   or

I spent   I gave the shopkeeper $30.00

$	c
15	00
+10	00
= 25	00

$	c
30	00
−25	00
= 5	00

So my change is $5.00

Making a budget

A *budget* is a plan showing how much money you have and how you plan to spend it.
People make a budget to spend the money they get for their goods and services.

People from many different communities make a budget.
Students can make a budget.

Take a look at Tafina's budget for one school week. She gets $150.00 each day. If you want to know how much money she gets for one school week you must add together the money she gets each day.

Monday	$150.00
Tuesday	$150.00
Wednesday	$150.00
Thursday	$150.00
Friday	$150.00
	$750.00

She gets $750.00 for one school week.

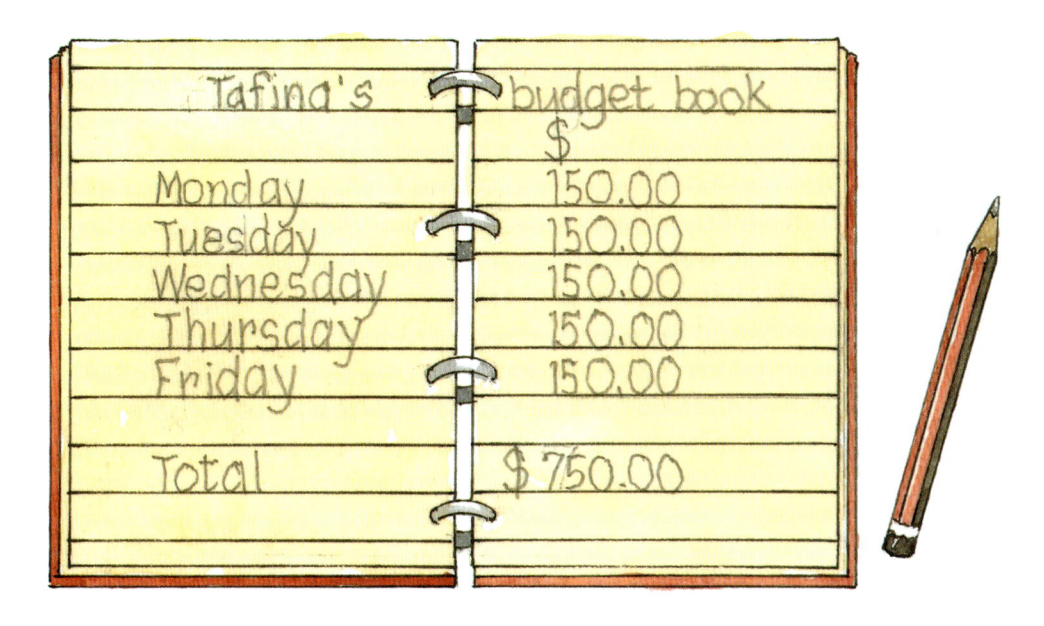

Tafina's budget book

	$
Monday	150.00
Tuesday	150.00
Wednesday	150.00
Thursday	150.00
Friday	150.00
Total	$750.00

She wants to save $250.00 to go to the movies with her friends on Saturday. Mom told her to make a budget. Here is her budget for one day.

Bus fare	$20.00
Patty	$35.00
Fruit drink	$40.00
Candy	$5.00
Total spent	$100.00

Daily allowance	$150.00
Total spent	$100.00
Savings	$50.00

If Tafina sticks to her budget for the whole school week she will save:
$50.00 + $50.00 + $50.00 + $50.00 + $50.00 = $250.00

This will be enough for her to go to the movies with her friends.

- If Tafina wants to save more money which item should she take off her list?
  Should she take off the candy or the bus fare? Say why you think so.

Adults should always make budgets. Some people do not make a budget and they sometimes spend more money than they have.
They have to borrow money and they get into debt.

Fractions

A fraction is a part or a share of something.

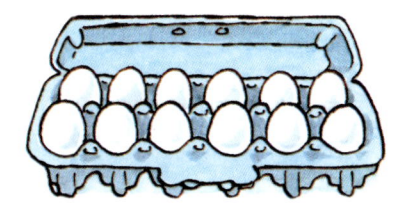

How many different ways can you share 12 eggs?

We can share the eggs in 2 groups of 6.
6 eggs + 6 eggs = 12 eggs

One half of the eggs is in each group.
$\frac{1}{2} + \frac{1}{2} = 1$

We can share the eggs in 3 groups of 4.
4 eggs + 4 eggs + 4 eggs = 12 eggs

One third of the eggs is in each group.
$\frac{1}{3} + \frac{1}{3} + \frac{1}{3} = 1$

We can share the eggs in 4 groups of 3.
3 eggs + 3 eggs + 3 eggs + 3 eggs = 12 eggs

One quarter of the eggs is in each group.
$\frac{1}{4} + \frac{1}{4} + \frac{1}{4} + \frac{1}{4} = 1$

We can share the eggs in 6 groups of 2.
2 eggs + 2 eggs + 2 eggs +
2 eggs + 2 eggs + 2 eggs = 12 eggs

One sixth of the eggs is in each group.
$\frac{1}{6} + \frac{1}{6} + \frac{1}{6} + \frac{1}{6} + \frac{1}{6} + \frac{1}{6} = 1$

We can share the eggs in 12 groups of 1.
1 egg + 1 egg + 1 egg + 1 egg +
1 egg + 1 egg + 1 egg + 1 egg +
1 egg + 1 egg + 1 egg + 1 egg = 12 eggs

One twelfth of the eggs is in each group.
$\frac{1}{12} + \frac{1}{12} + \frac{1}{12} + \frac{1}{12} + \frac{1}{12} + \frac{1}{12} +$
$\frac{1}{12} + \frac{1}{12} + \frac{1}{12} + \frac{1}{12} + \frac{1}{12} + \frac{1}{12} = 1$

15.7 The environment and recycling

How can we protect our environment?

Our *environment* is everything surrounding us.
In your environment you see many things such as buildings, trees, hills, roads, rivers, people and animals.

Many things happen in your environment. You may see people at work, shopping or playing games.

The people in the environment should help each other to care for and protect it.
A healthy environment will have healthy people.

Here are some things you can do to protect your environment.
- Dispose of garbage properly.
- Recycle plastic and other reusable materials.
- Take shopping bags when shopping so you use fewer plastic bags.

We should put garbage in a drum, so that the garbage collector can pick it up.
We should not burn it. We should not dump it in rivers or the sea.

Here is a song about litter. Sing it to the tune of Frère Jacques. Your teacher will help you.

Song:

    Bits of paper, bits of paper
    Lying on the ground, lying on the ground
    They make the place untidy
    They make the place untidy
    Pick them up, pick them up.

We need trees.
If trees are cut down we must plant new ones.

Why do we need trees?
We need trees to stop the earth from being washed away when it rains.
We need trees to help prevent the earth from drying out when the sun shines.
We need trees to keep the air clean and fresh for us to breathe.
We need trees to provide a home environment for insects and animals.
We need trees to beautify the environment.

> Discuss the importance of caring for the environment with your teacher and class.

Keeping our school and home clean

We all feel good when the places and things around us are clean and beautiful.
At school, we should begin by keeping our classroom clean.

Bits of paper, food, fruit seeds and skins should not be thrown on the floor.
They should be placed in the waste basket or bins.

At home we should have covered waste bins in which to put food peel and other waste material.
We should make sure that broken bottles, cans and woodcuttings are properly disposed of.

It is very wise to put waste in tied garbage bags before we put them in the large bins for the garbage truck to collect.

This will help to keep away the flies and rats.

We should also cut away bushes around our homes and keep drains clean, so that water can flow freely.

Mosquitoes love stagnant water. If we keep our surroundings free of stagnant water they will have fewer places to breed.

16 What are the places in our community that we find interesting?

16.1 Places of interest

Attractions

There are some interesting places and buildings in Jamaica.
These are known as *attractions* for visitors.

Some attractions are natural.
Some, like buildings, are man-made.
Some of these buildings are owned by the government.
Others are owned by private citizens.

Some places in Jamaica have very old buildings with an interesting history.

The old capital of Jamaica is Spanish Town.
Here are two of its old buildings.

Old Kings House

Cathedral of St Jago de la Vega

Here are some of the buildings in Port Royal.

Old Forte

'Giddy House'

Here are some of the other interesting places in Kingston.

Emancipation Park

Devon House

Bob Marley Museum

Ward Theatre

Page 93

Other parishes have interesting buildings and places too.

In St Ann, there is Seville, the place where it is believed that Columbus landed when he came to Jamaica.

In Rose Hall there is the Rose Hall Great House where Annie Palmer lived. She was often called the White Witch of Rose Hall.

Singular and plural

Singular means one and plural means more than one.

Many of the words you use each day will become plural if you add the letter 's' but there are some words that cannot be made plural this way.

You read some of these words when you learnt about your community.
Some of the words are 'community', 'city' and 'country'.

To make these words plural, take off the 'y' at the end and add 'ies'.

One	More than one
community	communities
city	cities
country	countries

Not all words that end in 'y' add '-ies' in the plural.

Here are some examples of words that end in 'y' that become plural by adding '-s'.

One	More than one
monkey	monkeys
donkey	donkeys
coney	coneys

Interesting places in your community

A place of interest to the children of the Ewarton and Linstead communities is the West Indies Alumina Company (WINDALCO) Bauxite Alumina Plant. The parents of many of them work at the plant where they make alumina.

The alumina produced at the plant is sold to other countries.
When the alumina is sold abroad money comes into Jamaica.
This money is called *foreign exchange*.

Foreign exchange is used to pay for goods that Jamaica buys from other countries.

> Where are the interesting places in your community? Discuss it with your teacher.

16.2 Natural attractions

Most communities have special areas that are called *natural attractions*.

Some communities are close to rivers, waterfalls, springs or ponds.

One of Jamaica's most famous waterfalls is the Dunns River Falls.

Starting on the beach, you can climb the rocks over which the water falls.

Other communities have caves, woodlands or cliffs close to them.

Some communities are surrounded by gardens or beaches.

People like to go to these places to relax and have fun. However, it is safer for children to go to these areas with adults they know and trust.

Nature dictionary

Word	This means...
beach	The land along the seashore nearest to the water.
cave	A large empty space hollowed into the side of a hill, cliff or underground.
cliff	A steep rock face.
garden	A piece of land on which flowers and vegetables are grown. It can also be a public park with flowers, grass, paths and seats.
pond	A small area of water surrounded by land.
river	A flow of fresh water through the land.
spring	A place where water comes up naturally from the ground.
waterfall	Water falling down a hillside over rocks.
woodland	Land with many trees growing close together.

Has and have

When we speak about one person, place or thing we often use the word 'has'.

Read this sentence.

Betty **has** a white puppy.

When we speak about many people, places or things we use the word 'have'.

Read this sentence.

The children **have** skipping ropes.

The word 'has' should be used with 'he' and 'she'.

He has long hair.
She has her lunch box in her bag.

The word 'have' should be used with 'I' and 'you'.

I have a big mango.
Do **you have** a pin to give me?

Jamaican money

Did you know that there is a picture of one of Jamaica's natural attractions on the one hundred dollar bill?

On one side of the one hundred dollar bill there is a picture of the Dunns River Falls.

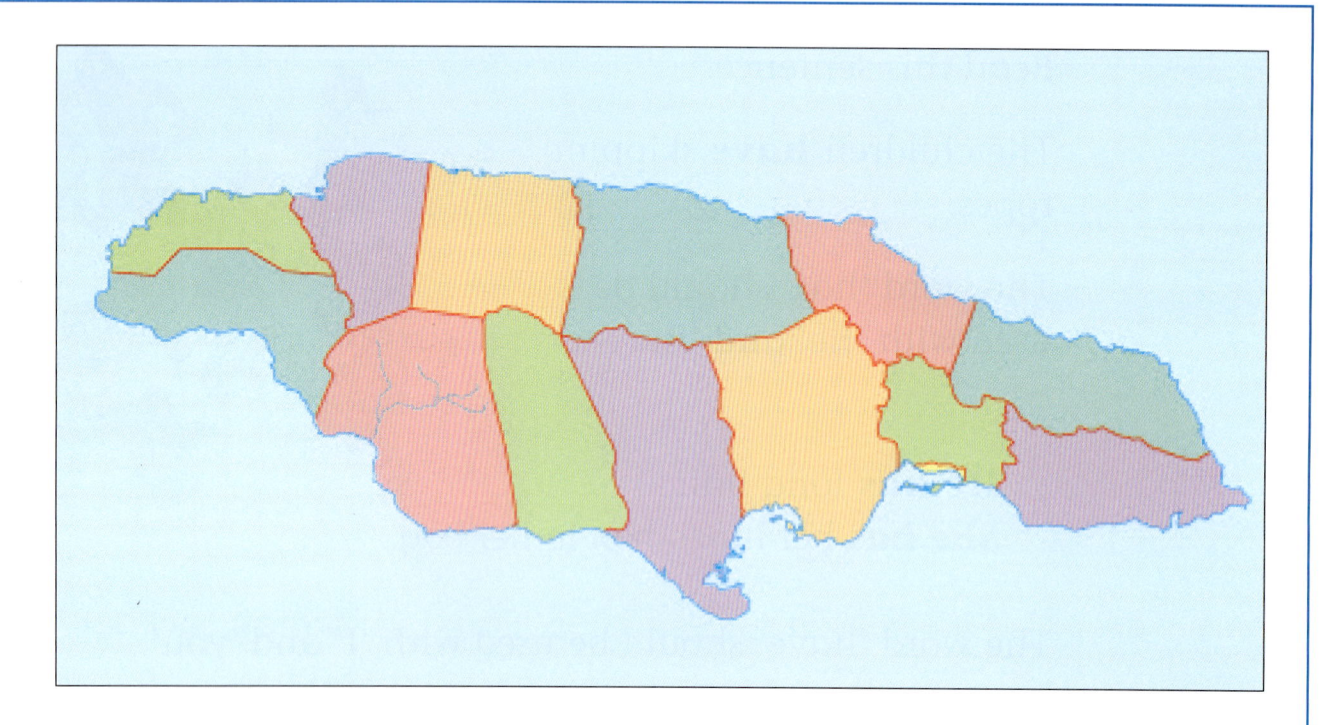

The Dunns River Falls is one of Jamaica's finest natural attractions.
It is situated in Ocho Rios in the parish of St Ann.

- Identify the parish of St Ann on the map of Jamaica.

- Identify the parish of St Elizabeth on the map of Jamaica.

- Identify the name of the main river shown on the map in St Elizabeth. Does it have any waterfalls?

Dicuss what you know about this river with your teacher and classmates.

16.3 Statues

Like a statue

A *statue* is a human or animal figure made out of solid material.
This solid material is generally stone, metal or plastic.

In Jamaica there are many statues.
Identify these national heroes from their statues.

Page 101

Page 102

Sculpture

A *sculpture* is made by cutting and shaping wood, stone or metal.
Clay may also be used to make a sculpture.

This is the Caribbean Sculpture Park in the grounds of the University of Technology.

Have you seen this sculpture or pictures of it?

This photograph shows part of the most recent and largest sculpture in Jamaica. It can be seen at Emancipation Park in Kingston.

The sculpture shows a man and a woman standing proudly, enjoying their freedom.

Words that sound alike

Words that sound the same but have different meanings are called homophones.

Read these sentences. Which pair of words sounds the same each time?

He hasn't got a hair on his head.

The hare runs across the field.

I got a pair of socks for my birthday.

She ate a pear for her lunch

We live on a busy road.

He rode the winning horse in the last race.

There are shops on the main street.

The horse has a very long mane.

Read this poem about the weather.

Poem:

Whether the weather be fine or whether the weather be not
Whether the weather be cold or whether the weather be hot
We'll weather the weather whatever the weather
Whether we like it or not.

- Name the pair of homophones in the poem.

16.4 Taking pride in our community

'A fi wi it, tek care'

This Jamaican saying means that we should take care of our community.

We can take care of our community by disposing of garbage carefully.

We should not destroy important things in our community.
Writing on walls and in public transportation makes them look ugly.

Drawings and writings scratched on walls and other places are called *graffiti*.

Paintings on walls are called *murals*.
They help to make our environment beautiful.

Are there any murals or graffiti at your school? Talk about how you can tell the difference.

Syllabication

We already know that words are made up of syllables, but do you know how to *syllabicate*?

When we syllabicate, we break big words into small units in order to call them.

Look at the word **activities**

If this word is broken into small units it would look like this:

ac / ti / vi / ties

If you look carefully you will see that each syllable has a vowel.

Therefore when we syllabicate, each syllable should have a vowel.

Syllabicate each of these words with a partner.

- Say the word and then say the word again more slowly.
- Count the number of syllables.

transportation   surrounded   community   dangerous

Taking pride in yourself

Here is a story about Kevon. If you read this story it will help you to tell the time.

Story: **Kevon's Day**

Hello! I am Kevon. I am eight years old and I am in Grade 2. This story is about how I spend my time on the days when I am at school.

I get out of bed at 6 o'clock. I go to the bathroom and take a shower.

By half past six I have washed and dressed. I have my breakfast.

After breakfast I brush my teeth, collect my school bag and set off for school at quarter past seven.

I arrive at my classroom by quarter to eight in time for devotion. We do a lot of work and we learn many things. It seems that break time comes very quickly.

I look at my watch and it is half past nine. This tells me it is time to have my snack and quickly use the bathroom. I never forget to flush the toilet or to wash my hands.

The bell goes at a quarter to ten and all the students line up outside the classroom. I am soon back at my desk. There is much more work to do before the bell goes for lunch at a quarter to eleven.

By this time I am really hungry so after saying grace, I eat my lunch.

We have some time to play before the bell goes at half past eleven.

We work until two o'clock when it is time to go home.

I get home at half past two and then I take a rest.

Sometimes I read a book or I watch television. Mother calls me for dinner at half past three.

Next my homework gets done and my dad checks it to make sure it is done well. Afterwards I sometimes read or listen to stories that mom and dad read to me.

By half past eight I am ready to go to bed so that I can be up at six o'clock next morning for school.

- Read Kevon's story again. This time as you read it, use a clock face to show the times when he is doing different things.

17 Why do we find these places interesting?

17.1 Tour guide

Story: **A Short Tour**

It is the beginning of another topic and everyone is happy.
We are going on a field trip.
We are going to visit some interesting sights.
We have a tour guide to take us around and tell us about the places.
We start our tour at Port Royal.

Port Royal is in Kingston.
It was the home port and look out point for the buccaneers long ago.
Port Royal was destroyed in an earthquake, and the port was buried under the sea.

One important place in Port Royal that we see is the 'Giddy House'.
We also see weapons that the buccaneers used to fight their enemies.

Next stop for our group is the airport.
We are all excited because we have a chance to go up into the tower.

After the tour of the airport it is time to go to Devon House.
We view the artifacts in the great house and learn about its history.
Last of all we get a chance to eat ice cream and play on the lawns of Devon House.

- Which part of the tour do you think the students enjoyed most?

Metres and centimetres

We use metres when we measure long distances such as the length of a playing field or the distance across a road.

Metres are too big to measure smaller distances like the length of a pencil or the width of a book. For these we use centimetres.

The short way of writing metre is 'm'.
The short way of writing centimetre is 'cm'.
There are 100 centimetres in 1 metre or 100 cm = 1 m.

17.2 Crops in my community

Some of our foods are grown from plants. Such foods are fruits, vegetables and ground provisions such as yams and potatoes.
These specially grown foods are called *crops*.

Here are some names of food crops:

banana   callaloo   wheat   nuts   peas   beans

Other food crops provide us with sugar, oils and spices.

Jamaica grows some crops for *export*.
Exports are goods sold to foreign countries.
These include coffee, citrus, bananas, pimento and sugar.
When we sell these crops abroad, the country earns foreign money.

Look at this map of Jamaica and identify the parishes where some of our crops are grown.

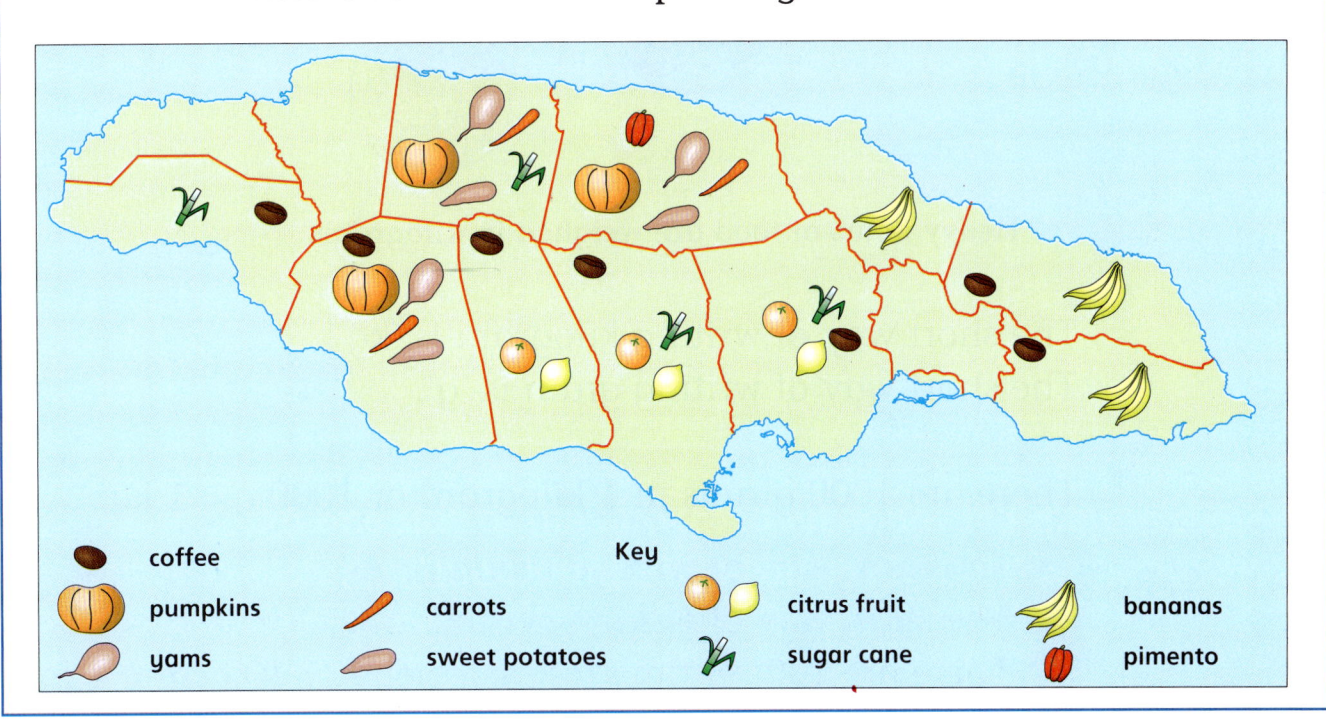

Key

- coffee
- pumpkins
- yams
- carrots
- sweet potatoes
- citrus fruit
- sugar cane
- bananas
- pimento

Page 115

Kilograms and grams

Look at these pictures of items of food we can buy from the market.

Light items of food are weighed in grams.

Heavy items of food are weighed in kilograms

The short way of writing kilogram is 'kg'.
The short way of writing gram is 'g'.

There are 1000 grams in 1 kilogram or 1000 g = 1 kg.

17.3 Nature walk

Story: **A Walk on the Wild Side**

Mrs Flowers' class went on a nature walk in the country yesterday.
The children were overjoyed.
They visited Mr White's farm.

A worker on the farm showed them many things.
They waded in a spring and they climbed fruit trees.
They even tried to catch fish.
They were also shown the blue mahoe tree, the lignum vitae tree and ackee trees.

They were lucky enough to see a doctor bird.

Did you know that the blue mahoe tree, the lignum vitae tree, the ackee tree and the doctor bird are all National Symbols?

There are / there were

Things that are happening now are in the *present*.
When we talk about them we use 'there is' and 'there are'.

Things that have already happened are in the *past*.
When we talk about them we use 'there was' and 'there were'.

Read these sentences.

There is a cat on the wall.

There was a cat on the wall.

There are flowers on the bush

There were flowers on the bush

17.4 Building a building

Our homes

Shelter is one of our basic needs.
People build shelters to protect themselves from the sun, wind and rain.

Shelters also provide us with a safe place to sleep.

Buildings in the past were made from natural materials.
Natural materials are those found in the environment.

Builders today use both natural and man-made materials.
Man-made materials are those that do not occur naturally.
They are made by people.

Many people are involved in the construction of buildings.
They include:

engineers   masons   carpenters   casual labourers

Past tense of words that end with 'y'

Some action words end with the letter 'y'.
To change these words to the past tense we change the 'y' to 'i' then add '-ed'.

Read these sentences.

I copy the work from the chalkboard.

I copied the work from the chalkboard.

I carry the groceries from the car.

I carried the groceries from the car.

- Say the past tense of bury. How is it spelt?
- Say a sentence using this word.

Fractions

A fraction is a part of a whole.

This bar of chocolate has 10 squares.

We can share the squares in
2 groups of 5.
5 squares + 5 squares = 10 squares

One half of the chocolate is in each group.
$\frac{1}{2} + \frac{1}{2} = 1$

We can share the squares in
5 groups of 2.
2 squares + 2 squares + 2 squares +
2 squares + 2 squares = 10 squares

One fifth of the chocolate is in each group.
$\frac{1}{5} + \frac{1}{5} + \frac{1}{5} + \frac{1}{5} + \frac{1}{5} = 1$

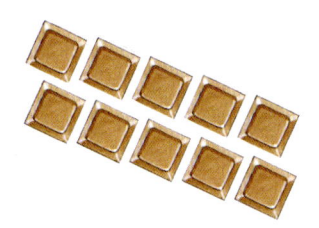

We can share the squares in
10 groups of 1.
1 square + 1 square + 1 square +
1 square + 1 square + 1 square +
1 square + 1 square + 1 square +
1 square = 10 squares

One tenth of the chocolate is in each group.
$\frac{1}{10} + \frac{1}{10} + \frac{1}{10} + \frac{1}{10} + \frac{1}{10} + \frac{1}{10} + \frac{1}{10} + \frac{1}{10} + \frac{1}{10} + \frac{1}{10} = 1$

17.5 Water in the community

A natural resource

Water is very important in all communities.
It is a *natural resource*.
People, animals and plants cannot live for very long without water.
Water can be a solid, a liquid or a gas.
Clean pure water has no taste, no colour and no smell.

In a community there are two main sources of water.
One is natural and the other is man-made.

Natural sources of water are ponds, rivers, springs and lakes.
Water collects in these when it rains.
The water in rivers eventually flows out into the sea.

We should all try to keep these natural sources of water clean by not dumping waste from animals and human beings, or any garbage from the home or community, into them.

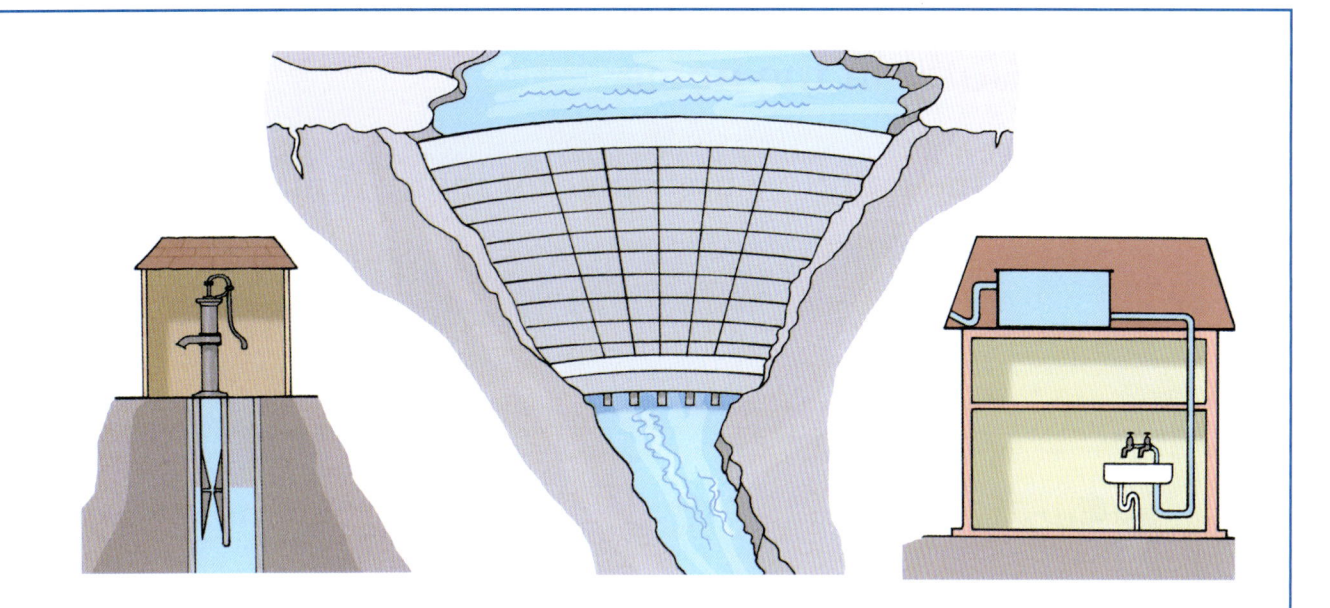

Man-made sources of water include tanks, wells and reservoirs.
The water comes from natural sources but it is stored and transported to taps for our convenience.

Water stored in the home should be kept in covered containers.

It is important to keep dust and insects out of stored water.

If you have flowers in a vase you should change the water often so that mosquito larvae do not develop in it.

You should not leave old containers lying around outside. Water will collect in them and provide places for mosquitoes to develop.

Water in the home

In the home we use water for many things.

We use water for drinking, bathing, cooking, washing clothes, keeping our home clean and to help plants grow.

In some communities people do not have safe drinking water.
They have to make the water safe to drink by boiling it or adding chemicals to kill any germs it may contain.

Here is a poem about water.

Poem: **Water**
W stands for wonderful liquid you see
A reminds us that we all need it
T is for that refreshing taste on hot humid days
E says every living thing needs water
R is there to remind us that water is life.
Beverley Dinnall

A great flood

Story: **Noah's Ark**

In the days of Noah many people were not doing the things that God wanted them to do. God told Noah to tell the people they would be destroyed if they did not change their ways. They all thought it was a joke and laughed at Noah. They even laughed at Noah when God told him to build an Ark, but this did not stop Noah from doing what God had told him to do.

Noah completed his Ark just in time. A pair of each animal went into the Ark. Noah and his family also went in and God locked the door. Then the rain began to fall. The people outside begged Noah to open the door but he could not.

The flood lasted for forty days and forty nights. The people and animals that were left outside all died.

After the rains stopped the Ark came to a stop on Mount Ararat. God did not like what He saw after the flood and so He promised never to destroy the earth by flood again. God sent a rainbow to remind us of this promise.

You can read this story in Genesis chapters 6, 7 and 8.

Rainbows

Rainbows are not just caused by rain. Sometimes we see rainbows in waterfalls, fountains, and even in the spray from a garden hose.

The light we receive from the sun is a mixture of different colours. The colours are:

red   orange   yellow   green   blue   indigo   violet

Drops of water can separate light into its different colours.

Some specially shaped pieces of glass also separate the colours.

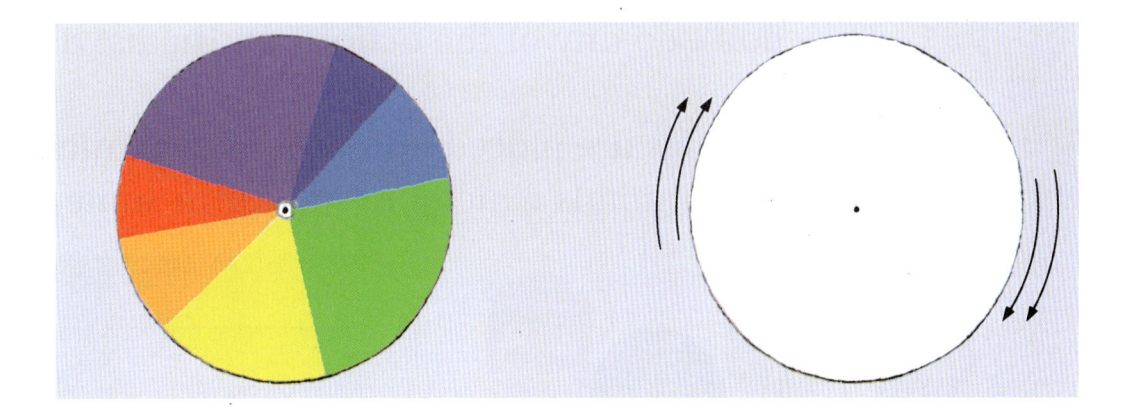

We can see what happens when we mix the colours by spinning a disc that has all the colours of the rainbow.

Page 127

18 What are the plants and animals in my community?

18.1 Plants and animals

Living and non-living things

In a community we find *living* and *non-living* things.

Animals and plants are *living* things.

This is what living things do:

> they grow
> they feed
> they breathe
> they get rid of waste
> they move by themselves
> they make young
> they are sensitive to changes in their environment.

Rocks are *non-living* things.
They don't do any of the actions on the list above.

Living things are placed into groups of plants and groups of animals which are similar in some ways.

Humans belong to a group of animals called *mammals*.
Dolphins are also mammals.

You might think that dolphins are more like fish than they are like humans but you would be wrong.
Both humans and dolphins have lungs to breathe air.
They give birth to live young and feed their babies by producing milk.
These are some of the *characteristics* of mammals.

Going on a field trip

Story: **Looking at Plants**

Suzie's teacher Mrs Simms often takes her class on nature walks.
She says that the fresh air is good for the children.
Today the students in her class will be looking at different kinds of plants when they go on their field trip.

Mrs Simms told the children that they would be looking at large plants and tiny plants.
They would also be looking for those plants that bear fruits for people and those that bear fruits for insects and birds.

'Hey, there is a tree with ripe fruits!' shouted Paula, running towards a tree.

'Don't touch that!' said Mrs Simms. 'Those fruits are good for the birds and other animals, but they are not good for us.'

'What a pity,' Pam and Marcia grumbled. 'And they looked so juicy.'

Just then Mrs Simms pointed to a tangerine tree laden with ripe juicy tangerines. 'You may eat the fruit from this tree, although the birds have started already. They are good for you,' said Mrs Simms.

Paula the brave one climbed the tree and picked tangerines for everyone. They really enjoyed the fruits.

Mrs Simms hurried them along because they needed to observe other plants to find out how they grew. A few metres from where they ate the tangerines they saw an apple tree.
Underneath the tree were baby apple tree plants. Marcia pulled up one of the baby plants.
Attached to it was a seed.

She ran with the plant to Mrs Simms. 'Miss, how can a seed grow into a big plant?' she asked.
'Well,' said Mrs Simms, 'Fruit trees grow from tiny seeds and if they are properly cared for, they can grow into healthy plants.'
'What does the plant need to grow?' asked Sam.
'The plant needs the minerals and water found in the soil. It also needs air and sunlight to make food.'
'Can we plant some seeds and see what happen Miss?' asked Susan.
'Yes,' said the teacher, 'That will be our project when we return to the classroom.'
The teacher and students had a wonderful time looking at plants. They had a guessing game about which fruits humans could eat and which could be eaten by birds and other insects.

- Learn how to spell these words. Ask the person sitting next to you to test you.

project   insect   nature   animal   human   observe

Verbs ending in '-ing'

Some verbs need help to make sentences correct.
We add '-ing' to some verbs to describe the action that is being done.

Look at these pictures and read the sentences.

The boys are playing football.

Mother is cooking dinner.

The dog is barking.

Mary is reading a book.

The words **playing**, **cooking**, **barking** and **reading** tell us about the actions that are happening.

Page 132

Plants in the community

All communities have a wide variety of plants.
Plants use air, water and sunlight to make their own food.
Plants have different textures, shapes and sizes.
They also serve different purposes.

Some are called *ornamental* plants. They are used for decoration.
Most plants are used for food. Farmers all over the country grow plants for food.

Food from plants can be sold in the communities where it is grown. It is also sold at markets and supermarkets in town.
In some communities plants are grown for *lumber*.
Dried and treated lumber is used to make buildings.

Animals in the community

Animals are a part of every community. They also serve different purposes.

Some animals are kept for food.

Some animals provide materials for making clothes.

Some animals are used to transport things.

Some animals are kept to protect us.

Some animals are kept because we like to look at them.

18.2 Animal sounds

Poem: **Animal Sounds**
God made animals
Both large and small
They make sounds
But they cannot talk
Some sounds are loud
Some sounds are soft
Thank the Lord
He saved them all on the Noah's ark.
Heidi Johnson

Animals make different sounds.

The sounds they make may be loud or soft, pleasant or unpleasant. In many cases, the size of an animal matches the sound it makes. Large animals often make louder sounds than small animals.

Here are the sounds that some animals make.

The lion roars.	The bird chirps.
The pig grunts.	The dog barks.
The cock crows.	The monkey chatters.
The bull bellows.	The bee hums.
The horse neighs.	The frog croaks.
The duck quacks.	The elephant trumpets.
The owl hoots.	The donkey brays.
The cat purrs.	The goat bleats.

Human beings can imitate the sounds of different animals.

Here are some words imitating the sound made by animals.

18.3 Growing plants

How are plants grown?

Plants are living things.
They live in many different places and environments.

Plants grow and change.
Plants need food to grow.
Most green plants make food for themselves.
To do this they use water and food from the soil.
They also use a gas called carbon dioxide from the air.
Plants make food in their green parts. They can only do this when there is sunlight.
There are many kinds of plants in the natural environment.

Some plants depend on others for shade and support.

Some plants grow from seeds.

Some plants grow from suckers, stems and tubers.

For plants to grow strongly, they need to be fed and taken care of.

18.4 Rearing animals

Animals

Like humans, animals need shelter, care, love and protection.

Some animals live in the wild and make their own shelter.

Some animals are kept by people and a home is provided for them.

Some farmers keep animals. These animals all have homes on the farm.

Page 139

Animals will become sick if they are not taken care of. They need to be properly cared for and their surroundings kept clean if they are to stay healthy.

Animal homes

We provide many animals with homes. Some of these homes have names.

Animal	Home
hen	coop
dog	kennel
horse	stable
pig	sty

Wild animals have homes they make themselves. Some of these homes have names.

Animal	Home
bee	hive
mouse	hole
spider	web
bird	nest

19 How are plants and animals useful?

19.1 Using plants and animals

How are plants useful?

Plants give us different kinds of food.
Most of the plants we eat are flowering plants.

Fruits such as oranges, apples and plums come from flowering plants.
Vegetables such as tomatoes and cauliflower are from flowering plants.

Sometimes we eat the leaves of the plants
When we eat lettuce or cabbage, we are eating leaves.
When we eat callaloo we are eating the stem and the leaves.

Often, we eat the part of the plant we call the root.
Yams, potatoes and carrots all grow underground. They are special roots that can grow new young plants.

We throw away some seeds, but some we eat.
Some seeds that we eat are peas, corn and peanuts.

Are plants really useful?

Plants have many uses.
Plants can be used for food as we have seen.
They are also used for shelter, clothing and medicine.

Wood comes from plants.
Wood is a part of almost every building.
Some houses are made only of wood, because the owners could not afford anything else.

Some materials come from plants.
Cotton comes from the cotton plant.
Linen comes from the flax plant.
These materials are used to make clothing for us.

Many medicines that the doctor prescribes are made from different kinds of plants.
Plants are even used for transport, especially in tourist resorts.

The bamboo plant is used to make rafts to take tourist on rides down the rivers such as the Martha Brae, Rio Grande and the White River.

Talk about some other things we use that are made from plants.

Local fruits

Everybody loves fruits.
Day and night fruits can be eaten and enjoyed.

The fruit vendors and the supermarkets sell all kinds of fruits.
Some people grow their own fruit, but others have to buy.

Some people eat fruit for a meal, while others use it for a snack or desert.

It is very important that we eat fruits because they are good for us.
Fruits provide us with vitamins, which help to keep us healthy.

Some fruits are available all year round.
In most West Indian islands you can get ripe bananas and oranges all year round.

Other fruits are *seasonal*.
This means they are only available at certain times of the year.
Fruits such as star apple, naseberry and jew plum are seasonal.

Many of the fruits in our country today are not grown locally.
They are imported from the Unites States of America.

How are animals useful?

Some animals provide us with food.

Page 144

Hens give us eggs and cows give us milk.
We turn some of the milk into butter, cheese and yoghurt.
We also eat chickens, pigs, goats, sheep and cows for meat.

The wool on a sheep can be turned into woollen jumpers to keep us warm. Its skin can be made into a sheepskin coat.
The skins of cows and goats are treated with chemicals to make leather for shoes and lots of other things.

Some animals like donkeys, mules and horses are used to pull carts but these are not very common in urban communities.

People sometimes keep dogs to guard their house and chase away people who should not be there.

Cats are kept to keep the house free of vermin like mice.

Some animals are pets. We keep them because they are interesting and we like looking at them.

Talk about some things we use that are made from animals.

Page 146

19.2 More uses of plants and animals

Musical instruments

Many useful things in our environment come from plants and animals.
Some musical instruments are made from plants.
Others are made from animals.
Some musical instruments are made from both plants and animals.

- Look at these instruments and say whether they come from plants or animals.

Page 147

Plants and animals as transport

Long ago animals were used for transporting people and goods.
Today we still use animals for transportation.

In some countries, camels and elephants are used to transport people and goods.
In many countries, rural communities use a donkey and cart or a horse and buggy as transport.

The buggy and the cart are often made from plants.

Boats and canoes are sometimes made from plants.

Plant and animal jewellery

Jewellery can be made from parts of plants.

The shell of the coconut can be used to make jewellery, utensils and ornaments.

Beads for bracelets and necklaces can also be made from plant material.

Necklaces, hair decorations and buttons can be made from animal shells or horn.
Purses and watchbands can be made of animal skin (leather).

Other things made from animals and plants

Did you know that feathers can be used to fill pillows and quilts?
Materials that come from animals are also used to make:

leather goods   fertiliser   gelatine for jelly

Did you know that plants are used to make paper?

Everything made from wood and paper was once part of a tree.
Even some rubber goods are made from the sap of trees.

Materials that come from plants are also used to make:

candles   paints   ink   soap   sweets   chewing gum

Plants are also used to make pencils and erasers.

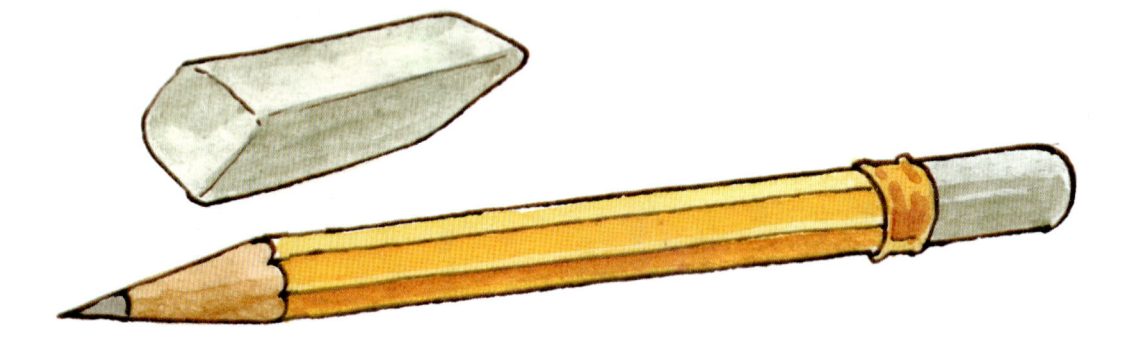

Talk about what a pencil and an eraser are made of with your teacher.

More about prepositions

Prepositions are *words that show the relationship* between one thing and another.

Some prepositions tells us where someone or something is.

Read these sentences.

The fish is <u>in</u> the water.

Father is standing <u>beside</u> the chair.

The girl is leaning <u>against</u> the wall.

The raft is going <u>under</u> the bridge.

Here are some more prepositions which describe where someone or something is:

on   above   below   behind   over

19.3 Healing plants

Plants and medicines

Some plants provide us with medicine.

We take medicines to get better when we are ill. Medicines are sometimes liquids and sometimes solids.

Medicines can be extracted from plants. Some of the plants used are:

mint

fever grass

peppermint

ginger

cerasse

aloe vera

Some of these plants are also used for flavouring food.

- Name an illness for which you would take each of these medicines to feel better.
  Ask your teacher and parents to help you.

Conjunctions

A conjunction is a *joining word*.

Conjunctions are used to join two short sentences together to make one longer sentence.

Look at this picture and read the sentences.

> I was feeling ill. I took a tablet.

Both sentences can be joined together to make one longer sentence.

> I was feeling ill so I took a tablet.

The word 'so' is a conjunction because it joined the two sentences together.

Read these sentences.

> I ran to school. I was late.

Now read this sentence and say which word is the conjunction word.

> I ran to school but I was late.

Here are some other conjunction words:

because   but   and   so   since   although   while

20. How do I care for/protect the plants and animals in my community?

20.1 Plants and animals in the environment

Environment

Plants and animals are a part of our natural environment.

They may exist in their natural homes or they can be adopted and cared for by people.
Like people, plants and animals need certain things to live and flourish.

Plants absorb water and minerals from the soil and carbon dioxide from the air. They use this to make their own food.

Animals drink water. They obtain food by eating plants and sometimes other animals.

How can plants and animals protect themselves?

Plants protect themselves:

... with sharp or stinging parts on their stems or leaves
... with the tough barks around their trunks
... with the poisons inside them.

Animals protect themselves:

... with the poisons in their bodies which they can inject into attackers
... with sharp spines on their skin that will stick into attackers
... by living in shells where they can hide
... with their sharp teeth and claws
... by camouflage so they look like their surroundings and cannot be seen.

20.2 Harming the environment

We must care for our environment or it will be destroyed and the plants and animals that live in it will die.

Here are two ways in which we can harm or destroy the environment.

Dumping domestic waste on open ground.

Cutting down trees and burning away undergrowth.

Here are two more ways in which we can harm or destroy the environment.

Spraying harmful chemicals in the air and on plants and animals.

Passing untreated human and animal waste into water and onto open land.

Disasters

Sometimes sad or unpleasant things happen in our communities and there is nothing we can do to stop them. We call these events *disasters*.

Natural disasters occur because of the way nature works. Some people call them 'acts of God'.

Earthquakes, hurricanes and floods caused by heavy rains are all natural disasters.

Ask your parents or teacher to tell you about a natural disaster they have lived through or heard of.

Some disasters are caused or made worse by the actions of people.

Cutting down too many trees increases the chances of an area becoming flooded.

Waste can pollute water supplies and attract animals like flies and rats that spread diseases.

Careless use of fire can burn everything in a dry area.

A great fire can be started by a very small spark. Sometimes hundreds of kilometres of forest can burn. Such a fire often lasts many days and destroy houses, animals and people in its path.

> Discuss with your teacher any great forest fires you have heard of on the television or in the newspaper.

A song about a flood

Here is part of a folk song about the flooding of a river.

Sing the song as a class.

Song:

>The river bed come dung
>The river bed come dung
>The river bed come dung
>An' a how yu come ova?
>
>Whai oh! Whai oh! Whai oh!
>An' a how you come ova?
>
>Me tek piece a long stick
>Me tek piece a long stick
>Me tek piece a long stick
>An' dash eena de wata
>
>Whai oh! Whai oh! Whai oh!
>An' a how you come ova?
>
>Me step pon de long stick
>Me step pon de long stick
>Me step pon de long stick
>An' a so me come ova.
>
>Whai oh! Whai oh! Whai oh!
>An' a so me come ova.

- Now sing the song again and this time do the actions.